DEAR COUNTRY

Dear Country
A Quest for England

HARRY REID

with photographs by
ANGELA CATLIN

EDINBURGH AND LONDON

*For Michael Fry and Jack McLean,
in reciprocal gratitude*

Copyright © Harry Reid, 1992
All rights reserved
The moral right of the author has been asserted

First published in Great Britain 1992 by
MAINSTREAM PUBLISHING COMPANY (EDINBURGH) LTD
7 Albany Street
Edinburgh EH1 3UG

ISBN 1 85158 374 2 (cloth)

No part of this book may be reproduced or transmitted in any form or by any other means without the permission in writing from the publisher, except by a reviewer who wishes to quote brief passages in connection with a review written for insertion in a magazine, newspaper or broadcast.

A catalogue record for this book is available from the British Library

Typeset in 11/13 Palacio by Blackpool Typesetting Services Ltd
Printed in Great Britain by Butler & Tanner Ltd, Frome

CONTENTS

INTRODUCTION		9
Chapter One	SO BRACING	
	Lincolnshire	15
Chapter Two	THE GLORIOUS AFTERTHOUGHT	
	Lincolnshire	29
Chapter Three	GIVE IT A REST	
	Major Oak	35
Chapter Four	BIKES AND BRAINS	
	Cambridge	45
Chapter Five	IT DEPENDS WHICH VILLAGE	
	London	55
Chapter Six	POTENTIAL UNLIMITED	
	Dover	71
Chapter Seven	EXTINGUISHED RESORT	
	Brighton—Hove	81
Chapter Eight	HEAVY FARE AND HEAVY AIR	
	Dorset—Somerset—Wiltshire	93
Chapter Nine	VERSIONS OF ENGLAND	
	The Vicar, The Brewer, The Publican, The Parliamentarian, The Club, The Commentators	111
Chapter Ten	BELLS AND BANDS	
	Ashbourne—Manchester	143
Chapter Eleven	FOX ON THE LINE	
	Crewe—Stoke	159
Chapter Twelve	DOWNHILL ALL THE WAY	
	Wigan—Preston	171
A NOTE ON TRANSPORT		185
PLAUDITS		192
SUMMING UP		194

This land of such dear souls, this dear dear land,
Dear for her reputation through the world,
Is now leased out—I die pronouncing it—
Like to a tenement or pelting farm.
England, bound in with the triumphant sea,
Whose rocky shore beats back the envious siege
Of watery Neptune, is now bound in with shame,
With inky blots, and rotten parchment bonds;
That England, that was wont to conquer others,
Hath made a shameful conquest of itself.

Richard II, *Act II*

INTRODUCTION

Like most Scots, I have an ambivalent attitude to England. I admire England's political and social maturity, its ability to create continuing, adaptable institutions, its long, rolling history, its magnificent literature, its ability to renew constantly in a uniquely stable context. I like the English; their courtesy, their sense of irony and understatement, their emphasis on privacy. I like their landscape, much of which is extraordinarily beautiful, though I think many of them have a false idea of it.

I also find in the English a certain blandness and complacency, and an occasional ability to be patronising. This last is not really a serious problem, and is in my experience mainly confined to sports commentators, of whom the English have produced a particularly raucous and arrogant variety. (I would make an exception of their cricket commentators here.) For such a polite and essentially decent people, the English can still inspire much dislike. I recall the great Welsh rugby guru, Eddie Butler, writing before the England rugby team's Grand Slam decider against France at Twickenham in March 1991. He referred to "the perennial problem of simply being English and the one team that the world loves to beat". This "problem" became even more evident during the World Cup in the autumn.

Again, I recall talking in Belfast, at about the same time, to the eminent Scottish sociologist Professor Steve Bruce, who surprised me by suddenly announcing: "I hate the English." Steve was talking here about meetings he'd attended at Stormont at which senior civil servants from England had struck him as arrogant, loud, ignorant and supercilious.

England is of course no longer the richest nation in the world, not even one of the richest; and though it still contains a glorious resource in its people, and their amazing diversity, it is undoubtedly finding it less easy to live with itself as a poorer, middle-rank player in the world. This has become the stuff of cliché; yet the loss of Empire has without doubt been particularly problematic. The consequent loss of externality has meant that England has had to look in on itself more and more, and it does not seem to be at ease with what it finds.

Thus, like most Scots, I have found much to admire in our bigger, more powerful neighbour; and also much that irritates, confuses and even worries. The traditional Englishman's attitude to his neighbour is one of restrained cordiality, held back by a fear of excessive involvement. The English and the Scots are technically more than mere neighbours; we are part of the same country, the United Kingdom. But culturally and socially we are to all intents and purposes two separate entities.

In this book I attempt, as (I hope) a reasonably well-informed and certainly sympathetic outsider, to discuss the condition of England as it is today. The bulk of *Dear Country* is a description of an intensive tour round England undertaken in the early summer of 1991.

I have visited England, with much enjoyment, many other times, but I have lived in the country only twice: as an undergraduate at Oxford for three years in the late sixties, and thereafter for eight months at Newcastle-upon-Tyne, when I was learning to be a journalist. (Two more different cities, incidentally, it would be hard to imagine. But they were linked in the public mind when serious rioting broke out in both cities during the long Indian summer of September 1991.)

Since 1969 I have worked almost constantly on Scotland's two most venerable newspapers, the *Glasgow Herald* and the *Scotsman*. This work has afforded me many trips to England which I could just about dignify with the phrase "of a professional nature". I have covered by-elections in Chester le Street and Manchester and Ripon; I have toured Windscale (now Sellafield) and the pits of North Yorkshire; I have interviewed a duke in his Midlands castle and interviewed a Spurs player, and his psychologist, in Enfield. I have travelled with the hard-pressed commuters of Southend and their redoubtable MP on the "misery line" to Fenchurch Street. I have profiled Manchester United FC and the professor of poetry at Oxford. I have visited Parliament and met many English parliamentarians. And so on, and so on. All this does not amount to anything of great significance—except to indicate that over the years I have been able to monitor the diversity of English life, and its changing mores.

My most interesting assignment, vis-à-vis England, came in the summer of 1977 when the deputy editor of the *Scotsman*, as he was then, Arnold Kemp, asked me to travel round England for a fortnight, and then write a series anatomising the state of the country. This was a somewhat mischievous commission, prompted in part by Arnold's wish to turn the tables on English journalists who were then frantically engaged in anatomising Scotland: it was the period when Scottish devolution was taking up much—for many English MPs, overmuch—parliamentary time.

Anyway, I greatly enjoyed this trip round England, although aspects of it were inevitably depressing. I predicted that there would be serious riots in England before long, and suggested that they would start in Brixton. When they duly came, a few years later, I—and I think most other people—were astonished that the first serious rioting occurred in Bristol. But Brixton, Liverpool, Handsworth, Bradford and other places quickly followed.

Dear Country

How would I compare England then and England now? Somewhat to my surprise, I found less nastiness, and less intolerance, in the England of the early 1990s than the England of the late 1970s. England was generally in a fairly placid state when I journeyed round it in the early summer of 1991. Eventually, as I say, rioting did occur later in the year in Oxford and Newcastle.

But if most of England seemed placid, I was made well aware of the tensions simmering beneath the surface. The most interesting and complex Englishman I encountered was the vicar of Langley, a run-down estate with quite horrendous problems, situated near Rochdale. This man, who came from a prosperous background in the south of England, still could not believe, after three years of dealing with people wracked by despair, that Langley was part of the same country he had lived in for the first forty-three years of his life.

Secondly, it seems to me now that Manchester rather than Birmingham is better placed to be England's Second City. In the 1970s I had little doubt that that designation rightly belonged to Birmingham.

Twelve years after that tour in 1977—by this time Arnold Kemp had become editor of the *Glasgow Herald* and I had become his deputy—I went to London to report for the *Herald* on the strains and stresses of living in the capital. The point of this series was to cut through the emotive envy-ridden platitudes about prosperous, pampered south-east fatcats, and look at the reality of life for many ordinary people in the metropolis; in many ways much much worse than it was in Scotland.

I have also visited England socially many times, and I have always specially enjoyed exploring the parts adjacent to Scotland: Northumbria and Cumbria. West Cumbria in particular seems to me full of undiscovered glories, containing as it does such characterful towns as Cockermouth and Whitehaven and that elegant little resort trapped in a time-warp, Silloth. These are places for the most part unvisited and consequently unappreciated by the hordes who congregate in the Lake District, a few miles to the east.

Also, since the winter of 1977-8, my wife and I have seen in each New Year with friends who have a cottage in the Fens, a few miles from Welney and right on the border of Norfolk and Cambridgeshire. I have come to love this strange, secret landscape—if you could legitimately describe such flat land, with such huge skies, as in any way secret. This visit has become a ritual, and the annual odyssey south, shortly after Christmas, has attracted almost mystical elements, particularly as we cover the last miles through the failing light, moving between the vast desolate fields towards Welney, through the tiny villages of Three Holes and Lake's End, listening for the melancholy honking of the Bewick swans as they seek the great wildfowl refuge, looking far across the sunken washes for the familiar lights of the pub at Denver Sluice, and then for the welcoming lamp outside the cottage at Hilgay Fen.

I should also mention that I have for long enjoyed the work of many of England's great writers, and one of the most rewarding aspects of the journey this book describes was the ability it afforded me to potter round some of the literary byways of England, seeking out places associated with the likes of Lord Tennyson and T. S. Eliot, H. E. Bates and William Blake.

I was aware that this is not always a happy pastime; I recall visiting some years ago with my wife, who is an ardent admirer of the novels of Mary Webb, the site of the mere which featured so largely in her finest book, *Precious Bane*. We found it wracked by noise as young men—early yuppies, I suppose—played with their loathsome power boats, shattering what remained of the Shropshire peace. But on this 1991 journey some gentle literary sleuthing took me to special places like Bag Enderby and Little Gidding, places that I would not otherwise have visited.

This preamble is not to suggest any deep or specially perceptive knowledge of England; far from it. It is rather to suggest a gentle and persistent acquaintanceship; and also that I have for a long period remained both curious and benignly interested as to the state of the great neighbour to the south.

Before describing the journey, I'd like to record how grateful I am to many people. To Arnold Kemp, a good and dear friend, for his consistent encouragement and support; to Bill Campbell, that paragon of publishers, for commissioning this book, and for endless good fellowship; also to Pete Mackenzie and Judy Moir for their patience, sympathy and succour, and to their colleague Lorraine for fielding my many telephone calls so pleasantly; to Angela Catlin of the *Glasgow Herald*, a supremely talented photographer; to Alison Brady, for her discreet and efficient secretarial assistance; to Bob Dylan, whose Bootleg Albums 1–3 came out just before I started the journey and whose wonderful songs sustained and consoled me as I negotiated England's costive traffic; and to the following people for taking the time and trouble to assist me in various ways: Terry Abott; Mike Addison; Yasmin Ali; Henry Blofeld; Roland Castro; Sue Clifford; Jill Crawshaw; Mike Cuerden; Martin Cullimore; Stephen Danos; Gill Dilley; Dr John Dilley; 'Doreen'; Roger Eames; Terry Egan; Kate Geraghty; Jean Gilbert; Rt Hon. Dr John Gilbert MP; Jan Glasscock; Terry Hamilton; Prof. Peter Hennessy; Leslie Illingworth; Dean Brandon Jackson; Susannah Jackson; Rev. Ian Johnson; Katie Jones; David McMurray; Andy Medhurst; Alan Midgley; Geoffrey Parkhouse; Layla Paterson; Geoffrey Skelsey; Sue Slipman; Lindsay Smith; Stephen Vizinczey; Rev. Henry Thorold; Dr Graham Walker; Wally the Tramp; and Stuart Yarwood.

Most of all, I should like to thank my wife Julie and daughter Catherine—special to me and special in their own right.

Harry Reid
November 1991

CHAPTER ONE

SO BRACING

Lincolnshire

I travel along the M18, a busy motorway, then turn east on the M180. It is deserted—a great swathe, three lanes in each direction, slashed through prime agricultural country. Not for the last time on this journey, I reflect that whoever is in overall charge of road planning at the Department of Transport—presumably not the various Ministers of Transport, they seem to change about once a year—is a mischief-maker with a sick sense of humour. Not for the last time, I am to cruise along a vast empty motorway, complacent in the knowledge that not too far away other roads will be clogged by traffic way beyond their capacity.

The M180, to judge by what I see on this particular day, when other roads in the area, motorways and non-motorways, are distinctly overcrowded, need never have been built. Why then was it built? I suspect as a feeder for Barbara Castle's Humber Bridge, the biggest singlespan bridge in the world—and also the local white elephant. After all, white elephants breed baby elephants, even if the gestation is protracted.

Dear Country

I reach the end of the M180 and head towards Louth. The roads become busy, but when I can, I scan the southern horizons, looking for the famous 295-feet spire of the great parish church of St James. Alas, I am virtually in the town before I see it. It is certainly impressive, rising elegantly from the solid tower that supports it.

I enter the church, and examine the booklets in the display area by the "common hutch". I am aware of a man hovering around in my vicinity; it is my experience of the bigger English churches that there is generally some buffer, usually an enthusiastic if amateur historian, lurking round the back of the nave, waiting to visit his expertise on the innocent tourist.

This gent is one such; but he is considerate, and says he does not wish to bore me. I ask if it is possible to climb the tower. He says the medieval door is locked, but he will get the key—if I promise not to be too long.

From the four sides at the top of the tower, Louth—which on the ground has seemed a rather close-set brick town—looks lovely, an orderly mosaic of red and green. The overwhelming impression is of neatness, of certainty, tidiness and propriety. I can see nothing that is crumbling, nothing that jars.

Then I hear the sound of a band playing below—a big bass drum, thump thump thumping, and bugles. I see a parade of scouts, cubs and other uniformed organisations far below, making its way through the narrow streets towards the church.

When I arrive back downstairs, they are filing into the church for their annual service. They are all very neat, very well behaved. I seek out my friend, and we have a chat before the service starts. When I tell him I am shortly to visit Lincoln Cathedral, his face darkens.

He is appalled by what is happening at this, the greatest of English cathedrals (a scandal of which more later). He says that for him, the real disgrace is that a lay conciliator—he emphasises the word lay—has had to be brought in to calm the warring factions in the Cathedral Chapter. "What will people make of the Church of England?" he asks. He does not say

So Bracing

anything about the present dean, but he tells me pointedly that the previous dean was an aristocrat.

He says he likes the sleepy nature of Lincolnshire. I mention that the road to Louth had been busy. "Yes, the roads are getting busier," he says. Then a pleasant if illogical afterthought occurs to him—"But we get very few Americans, I'm glad to say."

He asks where I am going next: Woodhall Spa, I say. Again his face darkens. Oh dear, he says, funny place, not at all like the rest of inland Lincolnshire. More like a suburb of Bournemouth.

(So many people are to tell me over the next day or so that Woodhall Spa is like Bournemouth that I determine to track down the provenance of the allusion. Henry Thorold, in the Collins *Guide to the Cathedrals, Abbeys and Priories of England*, quotes Sir John Betjeman describing Woodhall as that "Bournemouth-like spa in the middle of Lincolnshire". I later find the exact quote: "A further type of Lincolnshire scenery is the heath between the chalk and the limestone; in places it creates something as unexpected as Woodhall Spa, that half-timbered Bournemouth-like settlement among silver birches, heather and rhododendrons." So far, so good. But then in the Lincolnshire volume of the *Buildings of England* by Pevsner and Harris, I come across this passage: "There is nothing festive or glamorous about the spa, but there is about the town, which is mostly early twentieth century and much like a suburb of Bournemouth with tree-lined streets, pines, birches, other trees and shrubberies everywhere, and long affluent and soporific-looking houses for retired people who have not done too badly for themselves." So there we are. Either the comparison with Bournemouth was so apposite that it occurred spontaneously to both the knights, Pevsner and Betjeman. Or one of them quietly appropriated the comparison from the other.)

As I leave St James's, Louth, with the service in full swing, I noticed that a few (atheist?) scoutmasters are playing truant, sunning themselves on the benches by this fine church's ancient mellow walls.

And so on to Woodhall Spa, which may or may not be like the outskirts of Bournemouth, but is undoubtedly a curiosity. Promoted by East Lindsey District Council as "the Garden Resort", it does not have much in the way of public gardens, though there are plenty of large private ones fronting its villas.

It has a good golf course, a few hotels, a pleasant park—and an aura of ossified gentility. Its physical feel, with its pines and heaviness, reminded me of Royal Deeside, places like Banchory, Aboyne and Ballater. It also has the feel of a place where the elephants come to die. I saw an old couple sitting on picnic chairs by their car, so muffled and wrapped that you'd have thought they were in Siberia.

In the carefully tended woodland, you find the "Kinema in the Woods" and the "Tea House in the Woods". All very twee. I also found signs pointing to the Rheumatism Clinic; they omitted to mention that this facility has long since closed, as has the actual spa.

The place is self-consciously tidy; on the exiguous grass verges along the narrow road leading to the "kinema" notices warn: Ornamental Verges. Placing or Driving of Vehicles Prohibited. Penalty £20.

Woodhall Spa was created by the Victorians and had its heyday in the Edwardian era. It now possesses the drowsy slowness of a place reserved for old folk.

In one of its hotel bars, I had a conversation with a local who told me that it was a retirement centre for people from Nottingham and Leicester. But, he said thankfully, there was no spillover. By this he meant that it was not used by commuters to any big city, all the big cities being too far away.

After a laggard day in Woodhall Spa, I set off early the next morning the way I had come, to Horncastle. From there I drove deep into the wolds, Lincolnshire's chalky hills. Here are some of the most wonderful village names I encountered: Claxby Pluckacre, Ashby Puerorum, Bag Enderby. Here is territory that, if not exactly remote, is rarely explored and is unsung (except by the great Lord Tennyson). Here is territory that gives the lie to the oft-repeated canard that Lincolnshire is flat.

So Bracing

I turned left at Harrington, and moved slowly through magical, arcadian country. Past the thatched woodmen's cottages at Smackdown, through Fairy Wood and up a gentle hill, with Barn Holt and Paradise Holt sloping down to the left and higher slopes on the right. I arrived at the tiny village of Bag Enderby.

Here the peace was voluptuous; the intensity of the quiet was broken only by a distant wood pigeon and the bizarre screech of a peacock. A scatter of old houses and sheds surrounds the little church of St Margaret.

This utterly unspoiled building of local greenstone has stood since the fifteenth century, when Albinus de Enderby died leaving money for the construction of a church. You enter by an ancient wooden door. In the porch, a notice states: Lord Forgive Mankind, But Stop Him Using Sprays And Poison. As you step into this building, plain and austere but somehow very moving, an octagonal font, with an unusual depiction of the Pieta, is on your left. The short nave is freshened with flowers.

I snoop behind the curtain under the tower, where there is an old picture of the Queen and Prince Philip, and a battered Flymo. (The grass round the church has recently been cut.)

The service register notes that at evensong the night before there had been five communicants.

A hundred years ago, Bag Enderby had a population of seventy; now it is down to eighteen.

I step back outside the little church, gaze on the mature, undulating, wooded land and reflect that this, perhaps, is Arcadia. Even that constant curse of the English countryside, low-flying aircraft, does not succeed in disturbing my reverie for more than a few seconds.

Of course, the quietness has it downside. Depopulation is an obvious problem. Few visitors come to these parts; and those who do tend to come because of the Tennyson connection.

George Clayton Tennyson was rector of Bag Enderby and the neighbouring village of Somersby, where the rectory was, from 1806 to 1831. He and Mrs Tennyson had eleven children, among them Alfred, who became not just the greatest Victorian poet but also one of the most powerful exponents of the English countryside. In such a setting, their childhood should have been idyllic; but the rectory at Somersby was at times a wretched place.

This was because George Clayton Tennyson, although a brilliant scholar, was an erratic, aloof, self-absorbed man. He had "black blood" and was prone to attacks of depression so acute that it is reasonable to describe him as mad. He was also an epileptic and an alcoholic. As for Mrs Tennyson, she was kind to her children but she was easy-going to the point of disorganisation; she simply could not manage the household's affairs. And even something as basic as feeding such a large family required a fair amount of organisation.

The strains in this eccentric household were immense. The children were allowed to wear more or less what they wanted, what they could find; they were allowed to roam the wolds at night. Occasionally the tensions in the rectory drove the young Alfred to despair; he would run out to the welcoming blackness of the night, across the lane to the graveyard, and lie there wishing he were dead.

For all that, he was happier at home than he was at Louth, where he went to school when he was seven. He boarded with a relative, which was not too bad; but the masters at Louth Grammar School were sadistic and sarcastic; one of his contemporaries was in bed for six weeks after being beaten savagely for being slow with his lessons.

Alfred was bullied by other boys. Robert Bernard Martin, in his rewarding biography, recounts that Tennyson was surprised to find in later life that the most cruel bully grew up to be the kindest of men, while the only boy who protected him was later hanged for horse-stealing.

When Alfred visited Louth in his later persona as a venerable and distinguished man of letters, he refused to go near the school. But he remained intensely fond of the wolds, and their tiny villages. Much of his poetry is informed by his vision of this lost part of England; the lonely wolds, and beyond them the flat coastal plain and beyond that the cold, bleak, breaking sea.

From Bag Enderby and Somersby I drove round by Tetford and down through the soft hills to the plain by the sea. I had been intrigued, on perusing a 'Guide to the Anglican Churches of Lindsey'—an excellent booklet, edited by Roger Massingberg-Mundy—to find in it an incongruous advertisement asking *why compromise?* with your precious and well-earned free time.

It went on to extol the Richmond Holiday Centre, Skegness, with its leisure complex, heated indoor pool, spa bath, sauna, gymnasium, hotel, dancing, discos, late bars, live entertainment and carbaret with family room, toddlers' playsafe, recreation area. "Also included onpark is a supermarket, drug store, toy shop, sub-post office, betting office, cafe, laundrette, arcade, fish and chip shop, hair salon and doctor's surgery" (presumably this last for those who have overindulged in such a cornucopia of delights).

What struck me about this advertisement was, as I say, its incongruity: not what you'd expect in a scholarly historical guide to rural churches. But then the eastern strip of Lincolnshire contains a huge contrast: up in the wolds, there is quietude, down by the sea, there is—Skegness.

Skeggy is a remarkable resort. For a start, it has built its reputation on one essential characteristic: it is windswept, and proud of it. The great Skegness slogan, first promoted as far back as 1909, is *Skegness Is So Bracing*. The slogan was accompanied, in the famous poster by John Hassall, by an image of a jolly fat fisherman, throwing out his arms as he prances along the blowy beach. Now the Jolly Fisherman is the leitmotif of Skegness; he is here, there, and everywhere.

Another hero in the Skegness pantheon is Billy Butlin, who set up the first of his holiday camps here. Now it is called Funcoast World; the Butlin name is retained, although it is part of the Rank Organisation. Funcoast boasts, among many other attractions, an outdoor funpool (weather permitting).

Funcoast is just one of a long ribbon of holiday developments starting at the coastguard station by the Dunes pub, and stretching north: caravan parks (not yet known as funparks, but no doubt that will come), chalet parks (though chalets are increasingly regarded as old-fashioned), pool rooms, dance halls, discos, pubs, and amid all the garish glitter, the odd convalescent home.

Tennyson used to holiday at Skegness; he was regarded as an eccentric. A more recent eccentric was the Rev. Harold Davidson, who joined a Skegness circus in the 1930s after losing his Norfolk living. One day in July 1932 the vicar's performance as Daniel in the lion's den went terribly wrong; he was so severely mauled that he died two days later.

Skeggy has another claim to fame: it is the setting for a Booker Prize-winning novel (*Holiday*, by Stanley Middleton).

The resort's position on the eastern extremity of the vast eastern county of Lincolnshire accounts for its climate. Consulting the street plan and information sheet produced by the Skegness Publicity Service, I noted the following information:

Elevation—20ft
Area—4412 acres
Population—Resident 14,553 (summer visitors—80,000)
Water—8.1 degrees hardness
Air—bracing

There you are. Just like that.

When I visited Skeggy, the wind was blowing, sure enough. Yet a goodly number of people were walking the long sands to the south; children were enjoying their donkey rides; trippers were guzzling fish and chips. Yet despite this holiday activity the scene was somehow forlorn. An empty car screeched up and down the Big Dipper. The pitiful remains of the derelict pier jutted grotesquely across the beach.

Then the wind brought rain, and the holiday folk disappeared with great swiftness.

Soon the beach was bereft, and angry sludge-coloured water was pounding at the sea walls. As it darkened prematurely along the front, the only people to be seen were sign fixers, working on the coloured lights. As the rain intensified, I noticed a sign saying: Cars Displaying Disabled Stickers *Will* Be Charged. I moved into the town and saw, through the picture window of a home, a row of old folk, their trays in front of them, staring grimly out at the damp, desolate street. At first I thought they must have been looking at a television, but I could see the back of no telly. They were simply staring out into the street.

Skegness was beginning to depress me; but I received a warm welcome at the Vine Hotel, its oldest hostelry—where, almost inevitably, Tennyson used to stay. A bronze bust of the great man stands in the hotel's hospitable bar.

The next day, driving out of Skeggy, I saw a big yellow roadsign which told All Outward Bound drivers which way to go. I thought this was another "bracing" reference; then I realised they were just being kind, and guiding people out.

From Skeggy I headed west to Lincoln, and its indescribably magnificent cathedral. As you approach the city from any direction this stupendous edifice hovers, apparently just above the ground, a potent, enticing mirage. (The Rev. Henry Thorold, of whom much more later, tells of a Scot who was walking from Edinburgh to work in the Kent hopfields. As he approached Lincoln from the North, he walked down the long straight road that was once Ermine Street, and is now the A15. Always, the three great towers of the cathedral were ahead; never did they seem to get any closer.)

But when you do at last draw near, what had seemed to be sailing above the ground suddenly becomes, fixed; colossal, static, almost overbearingly solid. Inside, its quality changes once again; it is light and ethereal.

All is not well at Lincoln Cathedral; it never has been. It has been wracked by scandal and dispute throughout its long history. The latest problem concerns a fund-raising trip to Australia, undertaken in 1989 by one of the canons with the cathedral's copy of Magna Carta. Instead of making a useful profit, the enterprise made a huge loss—more than £500,000, although the Australians waived most of that sum.

This was in the time of the previous dean, an Old Etonian, the Very Rev. the Hon. Oliver Twistleton-Wykeham-Fiennes.

When the new dean, a blunt northerner called Brandon Jackson, arrived in 1989, he determined to find out exactly what had happened during the Australian fiasco.

The residue of his pointed inquiries has been bitter. The cathedral's chapter is divided, and Dean Jackson is an angry man.

As we chatted in the comfort of the deanery, Brandon Jackson spoke of the slackness that he was trying to root out. It had permeated not just Lincoln, but the entire Church of England.

"Our church has lost its way," he said. "It has become flabby and apathetic. Life has become far, far too easy. And the principal problem in the chapter of Lincoln affects the whole Church of England—freehold tenure.

"We simply cannot get rid of clergymen who are in the wrong job, or the wrong place. Not until they are seventy. The Bishop has asked canons here to resign; they have refused. A clergyman can openly defy his bishop when the bishop says: 'I want you to go'."

Dean Jackson then used a surprising analogy—perhaps he thought I had a boozy face. "A pub is only as good as its landlord," he barked at me.

"Freehold tenure is rotten," he continued. "But now it looks as if the synod, mainly fuelled by the unhappiness here at Lincoln, is going to abolish it, although it will take time."

(Fundamental change in the Church of England requires a two-thirds majority in each of the three houses: bishops, clergy, laity. Brandon Jackson thinks that if there is a stumbling block, it will be found in the house of the clergy.)

He told me that he and his colleagues wanted to be set free to minister the Gospel. "That has not been happening here. Things are in a very bad condition." He saw hope in the person of the new Archbishop of Canterbury, his friend George Carey. "At least people will know where he stands. They will listen, they will hear. Robert Runcie measured every word, so as to offend no-one."

Dean Jackson then told me of his visit to a charismatic church, the New Life Church, at the bottom of the hill (Lincoln Cathedral stands at the top of a steep hill. Everywhere in the town is known as uphill or downhill.) He was impressed by the liveliness, the enthusiasm, the spirit.

I turned to the fabric of the cathedral. It now takes at least £500,000 a year simply to maintain it. All visitors are "invited" to "contribute" to this maintenance, and the suggested donation is £1.50. (This is done discreetly, but the cathedral shop—within the cathedral—is frankly commercial. On its door a notice proclaims: Amex Travellers' Cheques Welcome. A red and yellow poster says: We Sell Kodacolor Gold.)

Given what is, in effect, a business transaction on entering the cathedral—no matter the euphemism about inviting visitors to contribute—there is a distinct element of shortchanging for people who come when a service is taking place, or about to start—say at 5 p.m. just before evensong. At such a time visitors are not allowed into the most beautiful parts of the cathedral—the great transept, the east transept, the Angel Choir and St Hugh's Choir (where the services are held).

There is obvious merit in this; after all, the cathedral is, supremely, a place of worship. On the other hand, if you charge a uniform fee, there should be a uniform return.

Of other English cathedrals, Ely charges £2.40, and St Paul's in London has started, for a trial period, a charge of £2.

But to return to the dean; I asked his views on the effective admission charge of £1.50. "I'm very unhappy about it. We consider salvation to be free. The average semi-pagan Brit will be happy to go to a castle and pay £2 or whatever. But you don't pay to go to church. Some people do resent it."

So I put it to him: he was the dean. Why did he allow this commercial imposition, if he so disliked it?

His answer explained the real problem of Lincoln Cathedral. Under its ancient statutes, neither the dean (nor, for that matter, the bishop) can over-rule the other members of the chapter, if they are in the majority. In other words, the dean is constitutionally unable to impose his will on those under him.

"Our statutes don't really allow anyone to do anything," he said. "You have here an equalising down. There has been a history of squabbles going back to the 1300s."

But Dean Jackson is frustrated by more than the constitution of the cathedral. He is frustrated by the building's very splendour. "It is almost a handicap to have such a wonderful building. I listen to the experts gathered at the fabric council. Experts in thirteenth-century statuary. Experts in medieval glass. Experts in gothic architecture. They will pore over a Romanesque frieze, discuss every detail with great concern.

"Oh, if only we as a cathedral paid as much attention to the souls of the people as we do to the stones, there would be a wonderful revival of religion in Lincoln and Lincolnshire."

This was said with enormous passion. He went on: "Some people say to me—hang on, Dean, they say, you ought not to sock it to them on Christianity. But I say: It's a Christian building."

Dean Jackson was happier when he told me about the prayers that are written by the public in one of the chantries. "A team of us work through them. I have some here: 'Dear God, help my T— through a difficult time. And help me through it too.'" Another was from a little girl praying for her dog which had been run over. And another: "I'm frightened of everyone . . . I might as well be dead. I can't make my marriage work or keep a job."

Brandon Jackson impressed me as a good man, a man of real spiritual power; but he is also, I suspect, a somewhat choleric personality who does not suffer fools gladly. I wish him well in his efforts to revive his church but—although I understand his misgivings about those who are obsessed by the fabric of his cathedral—I think he underestimates the capacity of the actual building to inspire.

Certainly, when I first stepped inside it in 1977 I felt almost transfigured, if that does not sound pretentious. And on this visit I could not stay away from it; I entered it on three separate occasions, dutifully paying my £1.50 each time.

I enjoyed a cup of tea in the Chapter House, served by two charming girls; the coffee house was closed, but that was a bonus, for there can surely be no better context in England in which to sip tea than in the beautiful thirteenth-century chapter house, where Edward I called one of his first Parliaments, to declare his son the first Prince of Wales.

I sat in the nave and listened to evensong being celebrated in St Hugh's Choir. I walked round the cloisters, and studied the grace of Wren's Library. I lingered in my favourite part of this sublime building, the Angel Choir, with its vast yet gentle proportions, and its profusion of noble stonework.

England has forty-two cathedrals; Lincoln is the best. Don't take my word for it. Alec Clifton-Taylor wrote that "probably, all things considered, Lincoln is the finest of our English cathedrals". Last century, John Ruskin was more categorical. He wrote: "I have always held, and am prepared against all comers to maintain, that the Cathedral of Lincoln is out and out the most precious piece of architecture in the British Isles, and, roughly speaking, worth any two other cathedrals we have." And William Cobbett was even more dogmatic. He wrote: "Lincoln Cathedral is, I believe, the finest building in the whole world. All the others that I have seen . . . are little things compared with this. To the task of describing a thousandth part of its striking beauties I am inadequate . . . ." Matthew Arnold, when he was in Lincoln, said that he "subsisted" on the cathedral.

I reluctantly left the cathedral, which was in danger of obsessing me, and walked round its purlieus. Here are old narrow streets with boutiques selling expensive chocolate, designer swimwear (surely not for Skegness), exotic cheeses, and pricey tourist knick-knacks of every description; there are also art galleries, antique shops, perfumeries; there are expensive hotels. There is a scented, breathless feel in the air; there is an excess of tweeness. It is like some ghastly upmarket bazaar; only the great cathedral, looming above all this, lends the upper part of Lincoln any kind of dignity.

I'd love to see the cathedral on a golden evening in high summer; or through mist; or on a muffled winter morning, when it is snowing hard. But these are for other times.

I walked down the unimaginatively named Steep Hill to explore downtown Lincoln. If uphill Lincoln is too twee, downhill Lincoln is dismal. Particularly depressing is the area south

Dear Country

of the station and west of the High Street, where the River Witham—dirty, meagre and sluggish—bends sharply to the south. Here is an unlovely mess of rundown factories, gap sites, partially demolished buildings, scabby patches of grass, derelict lots and pocked car parks linked by tatty terraces of brick houses.

The cathedral, floating high above, seems in another world.

CHAPTER TWO

THE GLORIOUS AFTERTHOUGHT

Lincolnshire

Before I left Lincolnshire I wanted to visit the man who should surely be known, if he will forgive the vulgarity, as "Mr Lincolnshire". To find the Rev. Henry Thorold I drove south, stopping only to look back, one last time, at the cathedral. I took the long and lonely minor road that leads through Brant Broughton and on to the trim village of Marston. Here, past the Thorold Arms and the Thorold C of E Charity School, you come to the gates of Marston Hall, home of the man the *Daily Telegraph* has designated as the "stalwart scholar-squire of Lincolnshire".

(I first met Henry Thorold in 1977. The rector of Sedgebrook, a village on the margins of the Vale of Belvoir, was smoking nervously at the entrance to the village school; he was waiting for Mr Thorold who was to open the village's summer fête. At last, an ancient grey Bentley swept past the rector. Mr Thorold and his aged aunt alighted. Dressed completely in black, apart from his buttonhole and dog collar, Mr Thorold exchanged a few preliminary courtesies with the rector and then delivered a stern homily to the villagers, urging them not to listen to those miserable fainthearts who were urging that the beautiful old churches of Lincolnshire should be abandoned. He announced that he had brought along six copies of a slim volume, edited by himself, on Lincolnshire Churches, price £1.50. To my surprise, they were rapidly snapped up. I approached Mr Thorold to ask him what role the church was playing in the controversy about the conservation of the nearby Vale of Belvoir, which was then raging. "Don't ask me about the Church, my man," he thundered. "I may be in holy orders but I have nothing, absolutely nothing, to do with the Church." Despite this unpropitious start, we then had a wide-ranging conversation about Lincolnshire, during which I was impressed by his great knowledge and the vehemence of his opinions. An untidy, shambling figure, he managed to combine an unkempt appearance with great dignity. Here, I thought, was a character of the old school.)

Henry Thorold's aged aunt died in 1982, and now he is supported in the splendours of Marston Hall by the Ballaam family, and in particular Faith Ballaam, "my treasure" as he calls her, "my head gardener, my flower arranger, administrator, cook . . .". Faith and her husband Karl, an engineer, live in the stable block, with their daughters Ruth and Marie. Together they keep the garden, as well as the hall, in excellent shape. "They provide great support to a decaying specimen such as myself," announces the Rev. Thorold.

He guides me round his garden, with its great 400-year-old elm, its huge laburnum (reputed to be the biggest in England) by the shrubbery, its gazebo, its high hedges. The River Witham drifts past, looking prettier than it did in Lincoln. He shows me his narrow avenue of high poplars; the trees were a gift when he left Lancing College.

After a couple of glasses of sherry by the fire, burning brightly though we are in the month of May, he conducts me round the Hall, showing me paintings by Joshua Reynolds and Poussin, by Peter Lely and John Piper. The Hall now consists of the middle part of a structure dating back to the fourteenth century: the wings were removed in the eighteenth century.

The Glorious Afterthought

I ask if it is the family home. "It's the oldest family home," he says. "We go back a long way. A Thorold was sheriff of Lincolnshire in 1052. It was through the marriage of Richard Thorold with the heiress of the de Marston family in the fourteenth century that the family first came to Marston. Sir William Thorold, who supported Charles I, was made a baronet in 1642. The ninth baronet moved to Syston, three miles from here, in the eighteenth century. That's where my cousin Tony, the fifteenth baronet, now lives. I'm merely the younger son of a younger son, though I do live in the oldest family home."

After this elaborate, if disarming, explanation, we decided to depart for lunch. We inspect the venerable Bentley in its garage, before setting off, in my car, across the border to Nottinghamshire, and an excellent pub called the Staunton Arms after the local landowners. "The Stauntons, good and dear friends, are an older family than the Thorolds," he notes. "Three hundred years older. I don't see how we can catch up!"

Through lunch, he talks away in his great rich voice, with the emphasis always on the final syllable. He calls the River Humber the Hum-baarr. He talks me through his life, and discusses the condition of England.

He was born in 1921. "I ought to have been born in Lincolnshire, but I was born in Mitcham. You know it? Horrid, squalid place." He was educated at Eton, Christ Church, Oxford, and Cuddesdon Theological College. From 1948 till 1968 he was master and housemaster at Lancing College, the Sussex public school. "I have no interest in education," he booms at this point.

His friend, the late Sir John Betjeman—John B, as he calls him—persuaded him to write the *Shell Guide to Lincolnshire* in 1965. When he was able to take up writing full-time, he wrote well-received Shell *Guides* to Derbyshire, Staffordshire, County Durham, and Nottinghamshire.

Then he was commissioned, by Collins, to produce what will probably be his most important book, the Collins *Guide to the Cathedrals, Abbeys and Priories of England and Wales*. He collaborated with another of his friends, the photographer Peter

Dear Country

Burton—among whose claims to fame is that he greatly annoyed the philosopher Wittgenstein with his loud piano playing at Trinity College, Cambridge.

The book was conceived as a companion to Betjeman's Collins *Guide to English Parish Churches*. It is a splendid guide, all the better for being quirky and idiosyncratic. Henry Thorold is a combative champion of the less celebrated English cathedrals, such as his beloved Southwell, and Rochester, just as he is a redoubtable champion of what he calls the "maligned" counties of England, among which he includes both Lincolnshire and Nottinghamshire.

The flavour, at once scholarly and chatty, of this delightful book can be gathered from the way he introduces Southwell: "Southwell is one of the great surprises of England, undoubtedly the least known of all our ancient cathedrals. 'Where is Southwell?' people will ask. And to the reply: 'in the heart of Nottinghamshire', they will look little the wiser."

Henry Thorold is chairman of the Lincoln Old Churches Trust, and he is on the fabric council of three separate cathedrals. He has worked tirelessly, and often successfully, to save and preserve Lincolnshire's many "redundant" churches.

He tells me he has just been approached by Lincolnshire Radio to air his views on the proposed new road signs for Lincolnshire's boundaries. "They are putting up those beastly notices all over the place. It's so undignified. You go into Nottinghamshire and you are told you are entering Robin Hood Country, whatever that is. I said, let's just call it *Lincolnshire* and leave it at that. That's simple, truthful, dignified.

"Do you know what they are proposing to call us? Lincolnshire, County of Yellowbellies. I ask you!"

But he was even more indignant about the alternative suggestion: Lincolnshire, County of Poachers. "We are not all poachers, though some of us may be," he intones. "You see, the English have become so sheeplike. One county does this, and they all have to do it . . . It cheapens everything. I told Radio Lincolnshire that I was quite horrified."

The Glorious Afterthought

England, he pronounces, has become—adulterated. "Enormous attention to money. Vulgarisation everywhere. The awful hold of the telly on the people. The English don't read any more."

Henry Thorold has no television set, no radio. No newspapers darken the door of Marston Hall. Even so, he is willing to ventilate his views to the media, when they contact him—which they do frequently.

He changes the subject: "If you come to stay and dine with me, as I hope you shall one day, I'll look out a silver ashtray I received in 1972, with a letter from Hoare's Bank, 32 Fleet Street. Do you know about Hoare's?"

"Is it like Coutts?" I ask.

"No, no, no. Coutts is just an expensive branch of the National Westminster. No, Hoare's was founded in 1692. I received the ashtray as a tercentenary souvenir. It is the only surviving, independent family bank. When I got the ashtray, I wrote back asking how long my family had been banking with them. I received by return of post a letter informing me that my account has been opened by Sir John Thorold, fourth baronet, on 30 July 1696."

As we concluded our chat I tentatively—remembering our first conversation fourteen years earlier—asked him about the state of the Church of England, and the particular unhappiness at Lincoln Cathedral. He said he believed that the church was doing well in the rural communities. He had no interest in the cities: England, for him, was the country.

"The rural clergy are working very, very hard. Our rector serves nine villages, eight churches, seven parishes. But last Sunday, at Marston church, there were twenty-five communicants. I think that is extraordinarily good for a small village."

As for Lincoln Cathedral, it had always been unhappy, he said.

Why? "Partly because of its curious constitution. The dean is not in control. It has been unhappy for so very long. I recall saying to our late rector: What is wrong with Lincoln? He said: 'It's the imp. It's the devil.'"

(According to an ancient Lincolnshire legend, the devil sent his imps out to make mischief. Two of them went to Lincoln, but they were so awestruck by the magnificence of the cathedral that they were scared to enter it. Then one of the imps summoned his courage, and flew in. He tripped up the bishop and knocked over the dean. He started breaking the windows. The angels told him to desist: he yelled back—"Stop me, if you can." And he was turned into stone, and condemned to sit for ever high above the Angel Choir. And indeed, high between two arches on the north side of the Angel Choir is a stone figure, grotesque, cross-legged, half-animal, half-human, with a leering, evil face and huge ears. This is the Lincoln Imp.)

It is, the Rev. Thorold reflects, almost as if there were a curse on the cathedral.

And so I took my leave of Henry Thorold. It would be easy, but wrong, to lampoon him as a dinosaur, trumpeting outworn notions so that they boom and echo across an old and ignored corner of England. There is both concern and pertinence in much of what he says. He may be an anachronism, but he is a kind man and a scholarly man—and he has worked nobly to celebrate much which, without him, might have slipped by unnoticed.

I also took my leave of Lincolnshire, a great county that is difficult to categorise. It is often, shamefully, overlooked; and when it is not completely forgotten, it tends to be tagged on as an afterthought. (An example is the *Shell Guide to English Villages*, in which Lincolnshire appears at the very end, almost as an appendage, way out of its geographic context.)

If Lincolnshire is an afterthought it is a glorious one. Of course, like everywhere in England, it has its tatty, grubby aspects. But I came nearest to finding Arcadia in Lincolnshire.

CHAPTER THREE

GIVE IT A REST

Major Oak

When I left Marston Hall I joined the A1 and headed back north towards Newark. I wanted to visit Edwinstowe, to examine the "Robin Hood industry" which flourishes there.

The Sherwood Forest Centre was quiet when I arrived; little sign of any "industry" here. An exhibition featuring "The Legend of Robin Hoode and Mery Sherwode" consisted of wooden figures depicting images such as "village life—toiling in the field" with a little elementary social history on the plaques. The final tableau was: "The king pardons Robyn" and the final plaque explained that Robin Hood (at last the orthodox spelling) was a common name in medieval England and that there were various contenders to be the Robin Hood of the Legend.

I passed a large outdoor sculpture showing Robin Hood and Little John fighting on the bridge, had a cup of tea in Robin Hood's Larder, and then visited the shop, which surprisingly offered various scholarly books analysing the legend. I bought one of them; when I read it later I learned that Robin Hood, insofar as such a composite character ever existed, was based not in Sherwood Forest but in that rather drab stretch of Yorkshire which the A1 transects north of Doncaster. Here, then, was a paradox: a tourist complex devoted to celebrating an allegedly local figure on account of associations which were tenuous, if not non-existent—and its own shop was selling material making that very point.

The shop, incidentally, sold a pleasing mixture of goods. There was a lot of kitsch, but it was inoffensive; some of it was even quite charming. There were Robin Hood masks, and bows and arrows, and the usual tea towels and mugs. There were also coal models of miners and pit scenes, a reminder that I was in the heart of the Notts coalfield. (If most of the Notts miners had not kept working through the protracted 1984–5 miners' strike, the miners would undoubtedly have won.)

I then walked through a delightful wood, in which there were many more silver birches than oaks, towards the Major Oak, which is apparently visited by 350,000 people each year, though I was quite alone when I viewed it on this late afternoon in May.

Many are the claims that have been made for the Major Oak, which was evidently named after an antiquary, one Major Rooke: before the nineteenth century it was known as the Queen Oak. Its age has been estimated at as much as 1,500 years, but modern scientific opinion is more sceptical. Indeed it is unlikely that it was even a sapling 700 years ago, when Robin Hood and his gang were supposed to meet inside it (the hollow trunk can accommodate a dozen people). It must have been, at one time, a magnificent and venerable tree.

Now it is pathetic. It is decrepit and forlorn. No fewer than nineteen big stakes have been erected to prop it up; and a large notice orders: *Give it a Rest*, explaining that the soil around the tree has been so trampled by spectators that water could not get to its roots.

Visitors were therefore asked to stay behind the fence to save the tree for the future. I obediently did so, once again wondering how such pleasant woods and such relatively narrow tracks could possibly sustain 350,000 visitors a year.

As I left, I noted that the whole area was threatened by subsidence, another reminder of the mining heritage; its real heritage, in fact. I passed Thoresby Colliery, adjacent to the village of Edwinstowe, and wondered if the future of England lies in tourism rather than the more macho, traditional heavy industries such as deep mining. Tourism is expanding rapidly; it is now England's second largest industry, while mining is contracting even more rapidly. Such reflections raise a much-considered conundrum. The question might be put thus: While it is obviously safer, and cleaner, to sell models of miners rather than actually to mine coal, is it more dignified, or for that matter more worthwhile? Or, to put it another way: Can tourism ever provide, let alone sustain, the camaraderie and the communal esteem that went hand-in-hand with coalmining?

The next day I journeyed down to Northamptonshire, to the handsome little town of Oundle. Scattered through it are the buildings of Oundle School, a typical English public school (fees £3,275 per term). The current headmaster, David McMurray, is a Scot. Tall, suave, with a perpetual glint of mischief in his eyes, he greeted me in his study and talked candidly about his pupils—and their parents.

He believed that "a sort of truce", which he reckoned had obtained since the beginning of the 1970s, was coming to an end. The 1960s had been a decade of turmoil for young people, and while he did not predict an equally stormy time ahead, he did see various signs of incipient turbulence.

"For a long time young people have been biddable, and extremely complaisant. But that is definitely beginning to change."

David McMurray then said that from his perspective, his school was on the borderline between north and south. I said that was surely wrong, from a purely geographic point of view. But he was talking about lifestyles. "I'd love to have more pupils from the north," he said. "There is greater prosperity in the south—there still is, despite current difficulties—but less social cohesion. Pupils from the north tend to be more direct, more straight. And while there is greater prosperity in the south, there is not, funnily enough, the same tradition of handling it. Handling wealth can be as difficult as handling poverty. A lot of people in the south of England have become wealthy very quickly."

On the other hand, he conceded that there was a certain dullness about pupils from the north. They did not challenge, they did not stir things up. Pupils from the south tended to be more mercenary, more streetwise, and altogether sharper.

I asked if there was any evidence that the coming decade was to be marked by the emergence of a new, gentler, more caring, generation. "Don't you believe it," he said. Many youngsters were self-centred, and had learned to become so from their families.

He then said—and I am convinced that he was utterly sincere in this—that he took no comfort at all from the perceived decline in the state sector, which had obviously benefited his and similar schools greatly. Many parents of pupils even at the supposedly best grammar schools—those that remained—were turning in desperation to the private sector. Yet such parents were reluctant to make the leap to full boarding for their children; they wanted day places if at all possible.

He said he was very conscious that he was profiting from the received notion of a decline in the state sector, and he was not particularly happy about it. Crocodile tears? I think not. He had obviously studied the problems in state schools, and was concerned about them. He said that in his view by far the greatest difficulty centred on what he called the "opt-out by teachers from traditional and important areas of social and extracurricular involvement." He stressed that he did not blame the teachers. "How could I? The pressures they are under are enormous."

Lest all this suggests that people like David McMurray can just sit back and wait for potential parents to come scratching at their doors, it should be said that the public schools themselves have come under considerable pressure to change.

During his seven years at Oundle, David McMurray has

established a reputation as the most reforming headmaster in the school's history. Among many other things, he has abolished corporal punishment and introduced girls to the school. By all accounts, the ambience is infinitely less strict and far more casual than it was a decade ago.

David McMurray then took me to lunch in the school tuck shop, where we were joined by three of his senior staff, and where we enjoyed, not crisps and ginger beer, but an excellent, traditional meal of steak and cheese, washed down by a first-class claret.

I asked about the "eccentric master", that formidable institution of the English public school. I was told that he had had his day. There was much reminiscence about one much-loved Oundle housemaster who would occasionally, in fits of rage, storm through the corridors of his house, lashing out at one and all with his cane. The pupils would scatter across the playing fields. That kind of thing could of course no longer be tolerated, I was told. No doubt, though it was not exactly what I had had in mind.

Evidently during the height of the Cruise Missile controversy (Molesworth air base is only six miles from Oundle) there had been a CND cell in the school, which had been tolerated if not encouraged. Some pupils had also formed OUT (Oundle Under Threat). But the consensus was that today's senior pupils were a pretty conservative lot.

This was confirmed for me when the senior history master, Alan Midgley, invited me to have a chat with a group of his sixth-formers. I found them courteous, forthcoming and articulate; perhaps they welcomed the unexpected ninety-minute break from their studies. We had a lively discussion, ranging from cricket to the perceived deterioration in the behaviour of younger pupils.

Very conscious that they were privileged, there was little radicalism among these sixth-formers. All were seventeen; not all of them intended to vote in the next election, and not one of them intended to vote Labour. One spoke passionately in favour of the monarchy; another decried the demise of Mrs Thatcher.

Four of them wanted to find work in the mass media; another wanted to make feature films. Two wanted to be lawyers. Not one of them sought a career in manufacturing industry.

They said—well they would, wouldn't they: their history master was listening—that their favourite subjects were History and English. Science was not popular; it was not well taught, and to some extent it was too much of a hard slog. A subject like history encouraged them to think for themselves. They felt that in science you were not allowed to think for yourself till university, or even beyond that. Oundle evidently had more historians than scientists in its sixth form; they didn't see anything wrong with that.

Most of them said they felt British rather than English (under some fairly persistent interrogation from me). They said they were patriotic about England, but on the whole they could not find a focus for this patriotism. They did think that it could be expressed to some extent through sport; some of them had, for example, taken enormous pride in England's Grand Slam rugby triumph.

They were, to my surprise, uninterested in cricket, which was reckoned to be a time-consuming and boring game. Tennis was the most popular summer sport; it was much more fun to play. Rowing was a growing sport, but one which could take a hold of you to the point of obsession.

They stated emphatically that no drugs were used at the school; but, as one of them said—we wouldn't tell you if they were. Their attitude to alcohol was ambivalent. They enjoyed drinking beer (they were allowed five pints a week) but they all regarded alcohol abuse as a growing and very serious social problem. They were conscious of strong pressures to drink outwith school.

They all insisted with great vehemence that young pupils aged thirteen arriving at the school were much more cheeky and challenging and generally difficult than they had been three or four years earlier. They were sincerely convinced that a sea-change in attitudes was approaching, and that a new, utterly rebellious, generation was on its way. Indeed, they presented themselves as the last of the old guard. Their master, Alan Midgley, was, however, distinctly sceptical about this. And lastly, they all agreed on something that tends to be forgotten in most discussions of boarding schools: that their experience of the school was far more dependent on the house they were in rather than the actual school.

Before I left Oundle, I made a few inquiries about possible "town and gown" tensions. The town certainly needs the school; it is by far the largest local employer. Apart from the hundred-plus teachers (who teach 880 pupils including eighty-five girls) there is a sizeable complement of domestic staff. For instance, as we sat down to lunch, David McMurray pointed out that throughout the town the school would at that moment be providing over a thousand lunches.

The town's dependence on the school could of course be a matter of resentment rather than gratitude. There were suggestions that the pupils tended to crowd people off the narrow pavements as they rushed round the town, but on the whole the relations seemed good.

I was moving on to Cambridge, but first I wanted to make two diversions; to nearby Little Gidding, because of its association with T. S. Eliot, and to Bedfordshire, which I had walked through exactly twenty years earlier.

Little Gidding is a tiny hamlet, set among broad green fields and small copses in gentle, undulating country. It is a secret place; a few trees, a few houses, and a tiny brick church, without a tower or a steeple. Inside this plain building the only garish notes are struck by the huge brass eagle-lectern—and the great brass candelabrum hanging above the little nave. A Christian community founded by Nicholas Ferrer in the seventeenth century was based here; its most famous, and most dangerous, friend was King Charles I. Defeated and desperate, the fugitive monarch arrived at Little Gidding on 2 May 1646—and then spent the night at Coppingford nearby. Soon afterwards he was arrested; Parliamentary troops came to Little Gidding, where they ransacked the little church, ripping out the woodwork and building a huge fire on which they roasted the community's sheep. The eagle lectern was thrown into a pond.

The community was revived as recently as 1977. Before then Little Gidding had been a place of eccentric and almost mystic pilgrimage; a few historians and contemplative souls had sought it out over the years. T. S. Eliot, an intensely religious man, was one of these. He was much moved by the place; and the last and finest of his *Four Quartets*, written in 1941-2, is called 'Little Gidding'. This great poem includes these lines:

> *A people without history*
> *Is not released from time, for history is a pattern*
> *of timeless moments. So, while the light fails*
> *on a winter's afternoon, in a secluded chapel*
> *History is now and England*

At the "parlour" in the house by the church the revived community sells mementoes. (Even in this most pastoral and numinous of settings there is a discreet commercialism.) I bought a book called *The English Spirit—The Little Gidding Anthology of English Spirituality*. It had a bumptious blurb: "Commonsense, simplicity, practicality, a suspicion of foreign extremes—and a fair dose of humour—are all the characteristics of the relationship the English have with their God—and all are to be found in the English Spirit." Despite this smugness, it proved an interesting and rewarding anthology.

And so, briefly, to Bedfordshire. In the summer of 1971, during a crapulous week in London, I suddenly sickened of excess and decided to walk through those parts of Bedfordshire and Northamptonshire celebrated by H. E. Bates. I had been reading *The Poacher*, one of his early novels, first published by Cape in 1935. This hard, gritty novel is the best exposition of the English countryside I have ever come across. It is a tough book, utterly devoid of sentiment.

Bates is now enjoying a revival, based on the successful television adaptations of the Larkin novels he wrote in the 1950s. But the real Bates, I reckon, is to be found in the novels and short stories he wrote in the 1920s and 1930s about the country in which he was brought up. There is, as yet, no "Bates Country". Eventually he went to live in Kent, and the Larkin novels are set there. But for me his best writing is about the Ouse and Nene valleys, where he wandered as a boy and a young man; I doubt if any other writer this century has evoked the physicality of the English landscape half as well.

That brief hike of mine in 1971 started at Bedford Station, where I got off the train from London. I walked westwards, through Stevington, to Carlton, a little village near Harrold. Not very far, only nine miles or so, but I was very hungover. That night I stayed at the Angel Inn, Carlton; my hosts were Mr and Mrs Stirling, who gave me much good conversation and, the next morning, a huge, sumptuous breakfast. I still have the bill for the B & B. It cost £1.50. After I left the Angel that day I had, in glorious weather, a long and grand walk through one of the loveliest parts of England.

I went along the Ouse valley to Felmersham, and then up to the long straggling village of Sharnbrook; on to Souldrop, where the landlord of the Bedford Arms introduced me to Greene King's wonderful Abbot Ale; I crossed the A6 and walked on to Knotting, and then over rougher country, across Yelden Wold, to Newton Bromshold, and finally, back on metal roads, round by Caldecott to Higham Ferrars, where I caught a bus to Wellingborough, and from there an evening train back to London.

This time, in my car, I approached via the A6 from Rushden. I turned off at Souldrop, where I dropped into the Bedford Arms for a nostalgic pint of Abbot Ale. Then I drove down through Sharnbrook to the Ouse at Felmersham, where I stopped for a brief walk. (At Oundle, I had walked for a mile or so along the banks of the Nene, a very different river. According to Bates, writing in his memoirs not long before he died, the difference is that between masculine and feminine: "The Nene is a straight and busy stream, utilitarian, unfrilled, not much to look at; the Ouse has a sort of womanliness about it, soft, indecisive, very beautiful, a broad bosom of a stream flowing through a country in which the very names of the villages are names coined by a soft-spoken and almost feminine people.")

At the old five-arch bridge across the Ouse at Felmersham, a little grass area had been landscaped to mark the Queen's Silver Jubilee of 1977. There was now, evidently, a country park at Odell, down the valley. Halfway along the road to Carlton, I came across the Daisy Bank Picnic Site, which had not been there before. The road was much busier. A lot had changed. Everywhere the country seemed packaged, organised.

At Carlton, now a very prosperous-looking village, I sought out the Angel. I had a pint of Banks's Bitter—slogan: Unspoilt by Progress—and I wondered if the bar was indeed unspoilt by progress. Coloured lights festooned the gantry. I inquired after the Stirlings; the girl behind the bar looked blank. "Long since gone," she said.

The bar had been expanded: it boasted a darts area, a juke box, a cigarette machine (the Stirlings ran out of cigarettes when I was there—I walked to Harrold to get some more for them), a pin-ball machine, and two fruit machines. Accommodation was no longer available. The Angel may well now be a better local amenity than that offered by the Stirlings. Even so . . .

CHAPTER FOUR

BIKES AND BRAINS

Cambridge

The first thing I noticed about Cambridge, as I was stuck in an infuriating traffic jam in Silver Street, was that it is very much a cyclists' city. Cyclists of all shapes and sizes on bikes of all shapes and sizes whizzed past the long line of overheating cars. I vowed then that I'd hire a bike.

I did so the next morning. Inquiries led me to Geoff's, near the youth hostel in Devonshire Road. Although it was a Sunday morning, Geoff's Cycle Hire was open. I was given a nice old-fashioned three-speed bike—no racer or mountain bike for me—which cost £4 for the day, plus a £20 deposit.

I set off to make its acquaintance in south-east Cambridge, the Hills Road/Mill Road area, before venturing into the university quarter, which I thought would be much busier.

It was soon apparent that Cambridge is a cycle-friendly city. For a start, it is very flat; nowhere is it more than 50 feet above sea level. More importantly, the county council has worked hard to make it a safe and suitable city for cyclists. Everywhere there are blue signs indicating designated cycle routes, and on main arteries there are "cycle reservoirs"—lanes where motorists are excluded.

But even in this most propitious of environments, cycling remains dangerous. There were 823 serious road accidents in Cambridge in 1990; more than half of them involved cyclists. As it turned out, the area I chose to "practise" in—south-east Cambridge—is the city's worst for cycle accidents. Because of this, the council and the Government have combined to create a new £2.6 million cycle route between Cherry Hinton and the city centre. This development includes a magnificent new cycle bridge over the railway, just along from Geoff's. It is an ultramodern structure, a "tube bridge" supported by cables hanging from a steel boxtower.

Despite this excellent record, the county council is refusing to rest on its laurels. Cyclists who wish to make recommendations or complaints or other comments are actively encouraged to contact Brian Oldridge, the council's "director of transportation".

I quickly rediscovered the joys of cycling, something I hadn't done for about twenty-five years. I cycled out to the new Addenbrookes site, at the far end of the Hills Road. Here is a huge hospital (then embroiled in controversy about staff cuts) and alongside it are the laboratories of the Medical Research Council, where some of the most important scientific work in the world is being undertaken by a team led by the Argentina-born Nobel Prize-winner Dr Cesar Milstein, the eminent molecular biologist who discovered monoclonal antibodies in 1975, a discovery which led to a world revolution in biological research, and will undoubtedly have profound and beneficial implications for the treatment of many illnesses and diseases, including several cancers. The site itself is vast but architecturally unimpressive.

Then I explored the colleges. Some of them were "closed to tourists" because it was drawing close to the exam season; but most were open. The students went about their business, apparently unaware of the gawping visitors.

I moved over the River Cam to the Sidgwick complex, a development on the west side of the town where some of the university's newer buildings are sited. I was seeking James Stirling's History Faculty Library, a celebrated but acutely controversial building which was erected in the 1960s. It was championed from the start by the great Cambridge historian Sir Geoffrey Elton but condemned by various outsiders, including the guru of English architecture, Sir Nikolaus Pevsner.

Stirling, like Sir Richard Rogers and Sir Norman Foster, is a distinguished architect who is much more fêted and appreciated abroad than he is in England. His current projects include an extension to the famous gallery he designed in Stuttgart; a shopping complex in Seville; a university in Singapore; a science library in California; and an art gallery in Milan.

I recall being entertained by academics at St Andrews University in Scotland in a building designed by Stirling; they mocked it mercilessly. Such philistinism, if philistinism it is, is fashionable; people who attack Stirling are quick to invoke the Prince of Wales. The Prince himself has attacked Stirling; and Stirling has fought back pugnaciously, even suggesting that the Prince is a rabble-rouser and comparing him (in this respect only) to Hitler.

The History Faculty Library is not easy to find. No sign points to it, and it is not sited alongside a road. Rather it is hidden away among other much less exciting modern buildings. A splendid temple-like confection of brick and glass, it looks from the south-east rather like a butterfly. This being a Sunday it was shut; the whole Sidgwick site was virtually deserted.

I eventually found a small sign by the door—as with most modern buildings, the entrance was not immediately apparent—which said simply: History Faculty.

Another spectator was prowling around, peering at the building from all angles. We fell into conversation. From his accent, I gathered he was an Irishman. He said the building was standing up well (at first I thought he was a pessimist, given that it was built only twenty-five years ago, but then I realised that it did not look out-of-time). He described it as "a great piece of sculpture". I said it was hard to find. He said that was typical of Cambridge: it was as if the university was ashamed of its buildings, old and new. He said there was not one decent, basic architectural guide available, detailing all the university's buildings.

He went on his way, but I remained, fascinated by this extraordinary building. I had heard that it was unpleasant to work in: overhot in the summer, too cold in the winter. But the more I looked at its exterior, the more interesting it became.

I noticed two external staircases, side by side. One led to a door; the other led directly to a brick wall. I was wondering if this was some kind of architectural mischief—a permanent, physical joke—when the door opened and a man came down the staircase. I asked him about the second staircase. He said that it had been bricked off when the new roof was built. The new roof was required because of structural and design faults.

I ventured that for all that, it was a magnificent building, at least from the outside. "That may well be," he said. "But—he *never thought about maintenance."*

I cycled back to Geoff's where I asked the man who took the bike back about the £20 deposit. Surely that was rather high? He told me that other hire shops in town charged much more—as much as £40. Theft was the problem, particularly with hires for longer than a day. He estimated that in termtime, as many as 10,000 cyclists might be on the move in Cambridge in any one day. It was, supremely, cycle city.

My bike ride had been, in a word, serendipity. I had really enjoyed it. Motorists had been polite, almost excessively so. Indeed, driving through the city the next morning, the perverse thought occurred to me that the cyclists were rather more careless and presumptuous in their road use than the car drivers.

Before I left Cambridge I went to the Old Schools, off Trinity Lane, to meet Geoffrey Skelsey, Assistant to the Vice-Chancellor. That modest designation describes the man who probably knows more about how the university ticks than any other individual. He is a fluent speaker, who walks as fast as he talks.

After a speedy scurry through the labyrinthine, apparently never-ending corridors of the Old Schools, we reached the Combination Room, where, over coffee, in deep comfortable seats, we discussed the university's past and present.

He denied that the university's constitution, and its relationship with the thirty-one colleges, was in any way obscure. He handed me a sixteen-page booklet entitled "An Unofficial Guide to the Organisation and Procedures of Cambridge University". (The first sentence reads: "The University of Cambridge is often thought to be an institution with unduly complex administrative procedures shrouded in arcane terminology." Having digested the booklet thoroughly, I have to say that I concur with the common perception: Cambridge University *has* unduly complex administrative procedures shrouded in arcane terminology.)

Mr Skelsey told me that, more than any other English public institution, Cambridge pulled itself together "after the long eighteenth century sleep". Since the 1850s, it had been able "disproportionately to represent" the intellectual trends of the modern world. I suggested that this was if anything an understated claim for an institution where, for example, the atom had been split and the structure of DNA had been discovered. Look at Cambridge's amazing list of Nobel Prize-winners, I said.

"Well," responded Mr Skelsey, "we do try to beware of empty hype. I'm not at all sure that we should concentrate on our Nobel Prize-winners. Some of them, after all, have only tenuous connections with the university." And he cited as an example the aforementioned molecular biologist Dr Milstein, who was employed by the MRC, not the university.

I countered by referring to the Cambridge biochemist Dr Fred Sanger, who is the only living scientist to have won the Nobel Prize twice (in 1958 and 1980) and the only chemist ever to have won it twice. (Fred Sanger is not a household name. One of the world's most distinguished scientists—and hardly anybody in England has heard of him. But then the English tend to choose unlikely heroes from their midst, and shun their real titans.)

Mr Skelsey said: "The point surely is that our admittedly lengthy list of Nobel Prize-winners can too easily become an obsession. Indeed it has become an obsession for some people. It is more important to emphasise solid, continuing achievement than the individual distinction of a relatively small number of people, no matter how pre-eminent they may be in their particular fields."

Nonetheless, I noted later that in what he termed the "boast pack" he gave me, Mr Skelsey had included the official list—and it is a very long one—of the university's Nobel laureates. And the pack further included the official information brochure for potential undergraduates, which highlighted this quote from a student: "It's very inspiring to read a book written by a Nobel Prize-winner one week, and then next week meet him or her in the flesh at a supervision."

Lest this suggests that Mr Skelsey and I indulged in sparring and point-scoring, I should report that I found our conversation agreeable and instructive.

He told me that although the university was attracting a higher proportion of the brightest school-leavers than any other institution in Britain, he was concerned that, for example, the cleverest youngsters in Tyneside and Glasgow might not include Cambridge in their plans. Much more work had to be done, although the admissions procedures had already been significantly changed to remove (1) the definite choice of a particular college by the applicant and (2) the university's separate entrance exam. The first was to prevent "old boy" or old school favouritism via a particular college; the second was to put the emphasis on the public exams used by all schools rather than the more recondite exams for which schools "in the know" could specially prepare candidates.

Even so, independent schools were still disproportionately represented, with only just over 50 per cent of the entry coming from the state sector. "That, however, is very, very different from forty years ago," said Mr Skelsey. He admitted that the proportion of women undergraduates at Cambridge, 40 per cent, was still too low, but that reflected another problem. The university was especially strong in the natural sciences and technology-based subjects, which historically, and unfortunately, tended not to be studied by girls. The university had not admitted women on equal terms till 1947.

Now there were no all-male colleges, and only two all-female colleges. (Later the university's information research officer told me about special summer courses which were being provided at the Cavendish Laboratory to attract more girls into science.)

"Nowadays," said Mr Skelsey, "our typical undergraduate will be reading engineering and will come from somewhere between Watford and Leeds, and will have parents who are either skilled workers or are in middle management." "Quite a big catchment area, both geographically and socially," I said. "Yes," he replied, "but it represents a real change, nonetheless. And the university no longer looks towards its traditional old-boy constituency."

He said that Cambridge now had far less influence in the Civil Service, and the professions other than law. "There used to be an assumption that the state did owe us a living. Arrangements would be made in the corridors of power by our alumni; you simply invited a few chaps down from Whitehall to a college feast, and so on. These days have gone forever."

I asked about Stirling's History Faculty Library. Mr Skelsey flatly denied that the university was ashamed of it. He said he thought that there had been a sign pointing to it, but that such signs tended to be stolen by undergraduates as trophies. The university had made a firm decision to spend well over £1 million repairing the building when its structural problems had become acute and it might even have been cheaper to take it down.

He told me that he thought the university was, on the whole, happy. "Certainly, campaigns which suggest that the universities are filled with embittered people who feel they have had a raw deal can be counterproductive." I asked if this was a subtle dig at Oxford; he conceded that it probably was.

"There is no doubt that Oxford, during the late 1970s and early 1980s, found itself in financial difficulties a great deal worse than ours," he added.

He then quoted a remark by Lord Jenkins of Hillhead to the effect that although Oxford and Cambridge were more or less equidistant from London, Oxford always seemed much nearer. The implication being that Oxford was closer to the Establishment; Cambridge was more aloof.

Mr Skelsey, while suspicious of "empty hype", was prepared to indulge in a little judicious and ambassadorial promotion of his university, if prompted. Fair enough. Cambridge University is one of England's few genuinely world-class institutions. It provides intimate and individually-geared teaching and a particularly flexible degree system, allowing for unusual combinations of subjects to be studied. It attracts leading academics—particularly scientists—from all over the world.

It has moved with the times; it has to some extent anticipated the times, in that it has consistently innovated. (An example is its science park, the first in England, developed over the past twenty-one years so that more than sixty firms are now based at an attractive site just outside the town, using university ideas to make things and create jobs.)

Perhaps the time has come for the university to sell itself a little harder; and indeed that would appear to be the rationale behind the recent appointment of its first information research officer, Susannah Thomas.

I chatted with her in her office in Trumpington Street. She told me that the university was very well integrated with the town; there were few of the classic town/gown tensions. She pointed to the fact that one in five of the students—a surprisingly high proportion—were involved in working with local people, through the Student Community Action project.

She ran through some of the more significant research projects being undertaken. The work on targeted monoclonal antibodies, under the direction of Dr Milstein; important research on earthquakes; revolutionary work on superconductivity; and so on. She cited two recent donations, of £8 million and £5 million from Mr Paul Judge and the Sainsbury family respectively. She referred to the recent appointment of a world expert on Aids and hepatitis, the French scientist Jean-Pierre

Allain, to be the university's first professor of transfusion medicine, and produced a cutting in which Prof. Allain compared Cambridge and Paris. Needless to say, Cambridge won hands down.

I left Cambridge with the sense of a dynamic, if abstrusely constituted, institution, set in an exceptionally pleasant, clean, history-rich environment. But the southern fens are also very flat, very cold, and very windy. In Cambridge the expansive gesture withers in the wind. The big claim is efficiently derided. There is a certain grimness about the place, a puritan coolness, a utilitarian determination not to overstate or get too excited. It is thus very different from Oxford, which tends to be a hothouse, metaphorically if not climatically.

Cambridge University is an elitist institution, insofar as it pursues excellence with vigour. But it is striving to build its future not on its inherited riches and the accumulated privileges of its great past, but rather on constant pragmatic renewal. It is one of England's success stories.

CHAPTER FIVE

IT DEPENDS WHICH VILLAGE

London

I was to meet my wife and several old friends in London. I drove in from Cambridge via the M11 (over sixty miles of motorway without a service area—another transport eccentricity) and down the congested Mile End Road, through the City, along the Embankment and across Chelsea to Kensington, where my wife and I had been given the use of a flat in Gloucester Walk, just off Kensington Church Street, by a company called In The English Manner.

Layla Paterson, who does PR for ITEM, told me: "Our flats and houses are all individually owned. The owners are away a lot and want to let them. We make sure that they are suitable for, and attractive to, visitors. They all have a homey rather than hotelly feel."

I asked Layla what was specifically English about the properties, other than their geographical location. "Well, I think of antiques and chintz, of bookshelves stacked with books, and nice comfy sofas. The English manner, I'd say means more cosy, less modern."

And that manner seems to please, for ITEM is doing very well, particularly with American bookings. The Gloucester Walk flat was delightful and, sure enough, there was some chintz, though not too much. There were plenty of books and a few antiques—and a very comfortable sofa.

We were there for only four days, but in that time we became very fond of the immediate purlieus. We particularly liked the cluster of little lanes and paths in the vicinity of the fine Church of St Mary Abbot, with its 278-foot high spire, and my wife was agreeably surprised to find a strong French flavour to the neighbourhood. (There are an estimated 50,000 French people living in London, and with both the *Lycée* and the *Institut Français* nearby, this is one of their favourite areas. There is an authentic *patisserie* in Church Street.)

London is of course an international city, maybe excessively so; but one of the benefits is that many little enclaves have been taken over and semi-colonised.

London is also a very fragmented city. Since the controversial abolition of the Greater London Council, it lacks an overall, city-wide elected body to speak for the city and to plan and co-ordinate its economic, environmental and cultural development. In some respects this has been a disaster; but a benefit has been that the localised character of the city has been even more concentrated; London is often, correctly, described as a long series of villages. Everything depends, of course, on which village you live in.

The area of Kensington we were in was posh, but not quite so posh as parts of neighbouring Holland Park—and not as dear as the other (eastern) side of Church Street, where the properties, in the vicinity of Kensington Palace, are among the priciest in London. While we were there, a flat in Kensington Palace Green was put on the market—at £13.5m. Yet less than a mile north is the utterly different All Saints area of Notting Hill, home of Carnival, and focus of much racial tension.

On our first evening we strolled down to South Kensington where we were to meet old friends, Stephen and Gloria Vizinczey. Stephen is a novelist who has established a world reputation on the basis of just two works of fiction: *In Praise of Older Women*, and *An Innocent Millionaire*. He is also a trenchant essayist; his collections of essays have provocative titles such as *The Rules of Chaos*, and *Truth and Lies in Literature*. He has had an extraordinary life. His father, a headmaster in rural Hungary, was assassinated by fascists when he was only two. When he was still a student in Budapest in the 1950s, he became a radical playwright. He took part in the uprising of 1956, and had to flee Hungary. After various adventures he arrived, penniless, in Canada where he started a new life. He eventually settled in London which he still regards, despite everything, as by far the most civilised English-speaking city in the world. His views on this and related matters are reported elsewhere in this book.

We dined at Daquise, an excellent Polish restaurant in Thurloe Street, which was filled with Poles, Hungarians and Czechs. Stephen said it was more East European than East Europe.

The next day I was to see Sue Slipman, whom I had last met in 1977 when she was about to take over the presidency of the National Union of Students from Charles Clarke. (Charles is now one of Neil Kinnock's senior non-parliamentary advisers. He is a burly, bearded man whom, in TV footage, you often see hovering behind Kinnock. But he was hired for his razor-sharp mind rather than his muscle.) That was a somewhat anarchic day at the chaotic Bloomsbury headquarters of the NUS; these days Sue is rather more austere. She is forty-one, and director of the National Council for One Parent Families, and I went to see her in her rather bleak offices, above an Indian restaurant, in Kentish Town.

I travelled up the notorious Northern Line—reputedly the worst underground line in the world, known to commuters as the Misery Line—three days after the chairman of London Underground had condemned his own network as "an appalling shambles, an infrastructure that had been neglected for thirty years". In fact I had a pleasant journey. The train was clean and by no means overcrowded; but then, it was not the rush hour.

The last time I had met her, Sue Slipman was one of England's most prominent communists. She eventually resigned from the party in 1980—"I should have left a lot sooner"—and a year later she joined the SDP. Quite a political journey in such a short time, I suggested.

"I had given up on the Left. In the late '70s I could see Thatcherism coming, and I wanted to defend the public sector. I got fed up talking to people in the Left with bone in their heads."

She stayed with the SDP, having stood as a parliamentary candidate in the '83 and '87 elections, right till the end; now she's a member of no party. I expressed surprise that she had not joined the Labour Party; she in turn was surprised.

"The Labour Party only started to change because of the electoral kicking it had right through the 1980s," she said. "My view has been and still is that unless it sets itself free from the trade unions, it is not going to develop a clear new role for itself."

Up until 1985 Sue was with the National Union of Public Employees. "I was working with very low-paid women workers—87 per cent of the membership of NUPE were women. They had 150 organisers. Eleven of them were women. It was a rough, tough male trade union culture. It was very difficult, almost impossible, to raise the question of where the union was going."

When she joined the Council, where she is in charge of a staff of twenty-seven, the public perception was that single parents were a social evil. The common idea of a single parent was of a very young unmarried girl, probably black and living in an inner city. Sue Slipman set out to "normalise" the concept of the single parent.

"In fact two-thirds of lone parents (the term she prefers) have been married and are single because of death, divorce or separation. Young teenage mothers are the exception." Sue Slipman is, incidentally, herself a lone parent, with a young son, Gideon.

Poverty is the biggest problem for lone parents. Only 20 per cent of them receive maintenance and 50 per cent of those who do get maintenance orders never receive the money. And the awards made by the courts—usually by male magistrates—are often derisory. The average award is £1,000 a year.

I asked Sue, the daughter of a Brixton taxi driver, about the current state of London. "A lot of people have simply given up on London. A lot of parents are moving elsewhere, including some of those who helped wreck London education in the first place. They are just giving up. There's a complete loss of confidence in London."

This disaffection was being compounded by incompetent local authorities whose commitment to obscure ideologies was wrecking any kind of social provision. "Just try living in Lambeth," she said. "Lambeth Council must be indicted, and indicted enormously. Education in Lambeth is run by loonies."

But then she made the point that in Lewisham, where she lived, education was much better run.

And that, again, is the point about London: it is divided and compartmentalised—educationally, politically, culturally, socially. Perhaps most of the world's megacities lack unity and cohesion, but you sense that at least some cohesion would not be too hard for London to achieve.

From London we moved on to the state of England. "In the late '70s, England was out of control. There was incipient anarchy. Mass demonstrations were able to influence judicial opinions. In these circumstances, Thatcherism *was* necessary." She went on to say that she had found much of Thatcherism painful, even cruel; but she would never deny that it had been necessary.

And so where was England, after a decade of Thatcherism? "English people now are not at ease with themselves. Many of them almost feel that they have prospered *too much* in a society which has become more divided. There are no opportunities for some English citizens, and an over-abundance of opportunities for others. And in some areas, Thatcherism has had no impact whatsoever. Our educational system was failing two-thirds of our children at the end of the 1970s. Ten years on, and it's still failing two-thirds of the children."

Sue said that England had still to grapple with the structural problems of its decline. She described it as a country "strung out" from a time when its imperialistic values were at once appalling and useful. It was finding it more difficult to run itself than to run half the world. It had lost externality, and could not cope with its new introspection.

The country had to confront the problem of vitality. The Thatcher era had undoubtedly released much energy and enterprise, but it had also produced unease, even guilt, because of the severe cost to some members of society.

"The English carry an enormous amount of history with them," she said. "They need to restore a national pride and confidence, partly based on history in a way that is not xenophobic."

A lot of food for thought there; I mulled over what she had said as I strolled through Kentish and Camden Towns, then round the perimeter of Regent's Park, and across Marylebone—my favourite part of London—to Hyde Park and Kensington Gardens. I had been thinking about what Sue Slipman had said, so I was not as alert to my surroundings as I should have been. I was, however, aware in Kentish and Camden towns of many Irish people lounging around with cans of lager and bottles of stout. While this may have rendered the atmosphere less salubrious than it might have been, there was no sense of menace. One Irishman, very politely, asked me for 20p. When I handed it over, he seemed astonished. Then his thanks were profuse.

I saw three quite well dressed old folk—they must have been at least in their sixties, more probably their seventies—walking along, engaged in gentle conversation. Each clutched a can of lager.

Again—these London demarcations. The moment I was in Marylebone, the cans of lager and bottles of stout disappeared.

Eventually I arrived at the Italian Gardens at the northeast corner of Kensington Gardens. It was a beautiful sunny afternoon and I decided to concentrate more on my surroundings, which were virtually deserted. I walked across the gardens to the flower walk by the Albert Memorial and then along to the southwest corner. Thus I moved right across the 275-acre gardens, which were extraordinarily lovely: sumptuous with pink and white hawthorn blossom, and the chestnut trees were in full bloom. And also, though it took my wife to draw my attention to this later, there was the distinctively English long grass with bluebells.

But—and this is in a way the most amazing fact I have reported about my entire journey—I encountered only nine people in Kensington Gardens. They were empty. Why? Surely not all Londoners are too busy to make use of their beautiful parks? Surely not all visitors are unaware of them? Or is the late afternoon just a peculiarly quiet time, a sort of interlude?

Had it not been such a glorious day, the absence of people would have been almost eerie. As it was, I felt indignant that so few other people were enjoying this pocket of arcadia in the great dirty city.

Early that evening I went to see Roland Castro, who describes himself as "an Italian Jew of Portuguese origins, born in Egypt and brought up in the Church of England". Well, who better to talk about the English?

Roland was one of the founding managers of *New Scientist* magazine in the 1950s. Then he left to start his own travel company, specialising in European city holidays. He built it up and now he employs forty people.

I had a couple of drinks with him in his cool, ultra-modern offices—a little piece of Italy in the middle of Belgravia. Although Roland describes himself as "the archetypal capitalist", he did not view the Thatcherite revolution of the '80s as an unmitigated success. He spoke with surprising affection of the former nationalised industries, which he recalled as providing courteous and hyper-efficient service. "I have no objection to nationalisation as such. Take the phones. They were always superb, most helpful if there was a problem. An engineer would be here at once. Now? BT are faceless and incompetent."

Then he angrily brandished a communication from the London Electricity Board. It detailed a forthcoming "supply interruption". The time intimated was 8 a.m. to 4.30 p.m., but "times given are approximate". There was a great deal of information on the form about deep freezers—what specific action to take to keep your freezer functioning. I noticed that, apart from a brief reference to water heaters, there was nothing at all about other domestic appliances, not to mention expensive business machines. I said this seemed peculiar. Roland thought it was worse than peculiar; it was insulting.

"My computers will be down all day. I'll have to get an emergency generator, and I'm not sure if I will be able to save all the computer memories." I asked if the board would pay for the cost of the emergency generator. Roland looked astounded: "They'd hit me on the head if I even asked," he said.

Here then was an entrepreneur, a businessman, being given just one week's notice that he was to have no electricity throughout a working day; and the missive which intimated this prattled on about deep freezers. I was not altogether surprised that Roland was affronted.

We then talked about two aspects of England: food and architecture. Although he insisted that there was not one place in London where you could get decent coffee, he conceded that the standard of food in English restaurants had improved out of all proportion, but it was still grotesquely expensive compared to prices on the Continent. He said that the recession was putting some bad restaurants out of business, and some of those that remained had had the decency to reduce their "outrageous" prices.

He said that young English people were lucky to see a great architectural renaissance going on around them. English architects were doing the most "wonderful, luminous" things, even with mundane materials like brick. I raised the controversial views of Prince Charles on architecture. Roland said that the Prince was obviously ill-advised. It was "typical, sad and pathetic" that so many English people didn't appreciate the new architecture flourishing around them. Prince Charles was giving the wrong signals.

That evening my wife and I met friends at the Stafford Hotel, off St James Street, for pre-dinner drinks. The hotel is obscurely situated and has a small cocktail bar. It was full of Americans drinking Fosters lager. The two bar staff—an English buffer of the old school and a young Frenchman—were quite overrun. The ambience was sticky, noisy and anti-social.

Then we walked round to a Japanese restaurant in St James Street where the admittedly excellent meal for four cost £200. Such prices are commonplace in the more upmarket tourist and business establishments of London, the "grockle shops" as I gather they are known. Indeed you can expect to pay at least £100 a head at the most fashionable restaurants. Anyway, we had dined just as well, if not better, the previous evening at exactly one-fifth of the price.

The next morning I went to Shelton Street, one of a network of lanes and narrow streets full of off-beat shops to the north of Covent Garden. Here, in small cluttered offices, the charity Common Ground is run. I call it a charity, which is technically correct—it is registered—but it has no membership and it would perhaps be better to describe it as a most original and innovative organisation concerned with England's heritage.

Since 1983, when it was founded, its two women co-ordinators, Sue Clifford and Angela King, have used Common Ground to pioneer a range of unusual environmental projects. But what they want to do more than anything is to "give people the confidence to stand up for what they feel strongly about in their own locality", as Sue Clifford puts it.

Sue is an academic planner who is on loan to Common Ground from the School of Architecture and Planning at University College, London. She told me she was desperately concerned about England's heritage: horrified at the way it was being "cannibalised" and "packaged". She wanted people to learn to be sensitive about the everyday things around them, the heritage of the future, and to give ordinary things house room, to keep them and cherish them. "We want to awaken people to the significance of the commonplace," she said. She was confident that people all over England had picked up Common Ground projects and found them exhilarating. So what were these projects?

Of those she described to me, I found Parish Maps the most interesting. The idea is for a group of people to get together and produce a map of their area, incorporating as much local knowledge, history and even folklore as possible. The actual map can be designed by an individual—a local cartographer or artist—or by a whole lot of people. It need not be final; it can be continually developed and replenished. The completed map can be displayed in a village hall, or a church, or a school or a community centre, and can thus stimulate further interest in the local environment.

Sue showed me several Parish Maps, quite a few of which had been successfully turned into postcards or posters. They were all completely different, and seemed to encapsulate a great deal of information with considerable flair and enthusiasm. Some of them were things of beauty. I was particularly taken with the Parish Map of Chideock in Dorset. Sue gave me the name of the project co-ordinator there, and I promised that I would look her up when I was in the West Country.

Other Common Ground projects include Apple Day, which grew out of an earlier Save Our Orchards campaign (6000 varieties of apple have been recorded in England, but only nine are currently available). In one of the great apple-growing counties, Devon, 90 per cent of the orchards have disappeared in the last twenty-five years. Another project is Tree Dressing Day, when people are encouraged to decorate and celebrate a tree in a particular street, playground, village or park.

Common Ground often works with local craftsmen and sculptors, as in another project, New Milestone. "We are interested in the cultural landscape. We emphasise the word place. We don't use the word site, or space."

I then discussed London and its problems with Sue. She comes from Nottinghamshire, but she has lived in London for almost twenty years. "I enjoy it and I hate it. It's alluring. But there is an overburden of confidence in London, and underneath there is the opposite. So much of London is now geared to tourism, and to being the financial capital of Europe. Yet every night I walk past people begging. A lot of them are young, a lot of them are women. Your heart is wrenched. I no longer give money, I have given so much. I think I am getting desensitised."

Like so many people in London, Sue bitterly regretted the demise of the GLC. "That was quite monstrous. London now has no strategic authority, to plan transport, for example. Transport in London is dire. It's desperate. London is beginning to feel like an island, separate from the rest of England. But a lot of the people have made it like that, the power people, the politicians, people in the media, the engineers of change— so many of them also have their place out of town, where they behave quite differently."

Yet Sue Clifford was at pains to emphasise positive aspects of London as well. "I just step into Shelton Street and I am among such happy, friendly, chatty people, many of them of Italian origin."

I asked if London needed a counterpoint—a real Second City to weigh against the pull to the southeast. She said that she thought that Manchester was beginning to assert itself, and could perhaps in time fulfil that role.

I left enthusiastic about Common Ground. It is a small organisation—the annual income is less than £200,000—and it has a very English, marginally eccentric air about it. But it is a necessary antidote to the packagers, the commercialisers, the cleaners-up and the other busybodies of the English heritage industry, and I wish it well.

That evening I was to visit Doreen, a woman whose husband walked out on her three years ago, leaving her to bring up two young children as well as support her mother. I had been put in touch with her through the National Council for One Parent Families. Her story was all too typical of how abandoned mothers are treated by English bureaucrats.

I arrived slightly early at her house near Kew Bridge—she didn't want me to come to the house until the children were asleep—and so I looked round the vicinity. It was not pretty.

It could and should have been one of the loveliest stretches of the Thames. Kew Gardens were just across the river. But the river itself was indescribably filthy. Squalid flotsam was drifting slowly in the direction of the sea. First it would have to float past Docklands, that apotheosis of the new London. It was low tide, and all sorts of litter and old masonry and other rubbish scarred the mudflats. Slogans were sprayed across the doors of Horseferry Rowing Club. On a sad little strip of grass by the river, opposite Kew Gardens Pier, a group of cubs were busy erecting a blue tent. The bridge was clogged with barely moving traffic, inching forward in each direction, although it was after 8 p.m.

Doreen lives in her little house, which she has had to re-mortgage, with her elderly mother, and her daughter Annika, who is almost six, and her son James, who is almost three.

She is a lively, even vivacious personality. She had a good job with an oil company in North Africa, which was where she met her husband, a Swede. They were happy enough there. They were married when she was thirty-eight, and pregnant. "I should have followed my gut instinct—it was not to get married."

When her husband walked out on her, she had several "terrible" months. She broke down in a DSS office. "I'd seen some bad places, like border posts between Libya and Tunisia, but this was the worst place I had ever been. Everybody was so rundown, so desperate. They said to me that whatever they paid me, they would claim back from my husband. I gave them all the information I had. They wrote two letters and then they gave up. I found that incredible. I took me five months to realise that nobody there would help me."

Doreen had already determined to bring up her two children by her own efforts. She hired a private detective to track down her husband; she had a rough idea that he'd gone to Cumbria.

She found the private eye most supportive, much more helpful than the people at the DSS. He traced her husband,

and then assisted her when she instigated court proceedings, in Cumbria, for the maintenance of her children. The court awarded her £50 per week for each child. (Her solicitor had told her she would be very lucky to get £10 a week. She replied that her children were worth more than £10 a week.)

Her husband did not appear in court and the original award was merely an interim order. The husband did appear at the next hearing, and the order was then cut by half. The magistrate asked Doreen if she had a television. He also asked if she had a telephone. As she says, he did not ask how she did her shopping, "which was by bus carrying a baby in a push chair and holding onto a toddler".

Despite the two court orders, Doreen did not actually receive any payments. She eventually requested that the court issue a warrant for non-payment of maintenance. An attachment order was issued, and at last payments began to come through—irregularly. While all this had been going on, the DSS had point blank refused to accept that she was not getting maintenance. She had to lodge an official appeal; it was duly upheld.

When the money started coming in Doreen set about finding a permanent job and someone to look after her children. She found a carer, and started a temporary job in October 1989. The carer left suddenly in February 1990. Doreen had to quit her job at once. Eventually she found a place for her son at a private nursery, at £50 a week. Her daughter was by this time at school. She then found another temporary job, with Hammersmith and Fulham Council; this later became permanent.

Meanwhile the maintenance payments had slipped to a total of £38. Furthermore, the court in Cumbria had issued a summons on a variation order, asking for an official reduction in the payments, although she had good reason to believe that her husband was spending a lot of money buying a pub.

When I spoke to Doreen, she was dreading the disruption, and cost, of having to journey up to Cumbria to fight the variation order.

"I have no regard for English justice," she told me. "In fact, I am disgusted. I don't think anyone owes me anything apart from my husband, but no-one is interested in helping me—certainly not any of the state agencies.

"England is back in the Dark Ages. The courts are sexist. In Sweden, where my husband comes from, it is all so different. An official solicitor sorts everything out. A maintenance sum is decided, and paid by the local social security office. This set amount can never be interrupted for any reason whatsoever. It is up to the state to get the money from the husband. That is the right kind of system. That is fair."

Doreen then said that if her maintenance was cut again, she was going to take her two children to Sweden. "I don't want to go, though it's a lot cleaner than here. But it's the only way I could bring up my children properly."

Over several cups of tea, Doreen talked me through her day. She always gets up between five and six, when she makes a packed lunch for herself and her daughter. Then she does the housework and ironing. "I have some time to myself then. It helps me face the day." Then she gets the children up and gives them breakfast. The three of them are ready to leave soon after 8.00.

In the evenings she tries to leave her work by 5.15, though this is not always possible. She tries to be home by 6.00. She feels that she can't leave her mother, who is over seventy, to look after the children for any longer. Either she or her mother cooks the evening meal, and then the children are bathed and put to bed. She looks out their clothes for the next day. By this time she is exhausted.

But not as exhausted as she is on Sunday nights, after two days, non-stop, with the children. "In a way I am glad to get back to work on Monday. The kids are so active and noisy. I am definitely too old for this."

She has two brothers who help her financially. "My family have been very good. To be honest, they have clothed the children. And my sister-in-law will occasionally take the kids overnight." Doreen has a lot of friends, but she is too tired to enjoy a proper night out.

At times, she becomes immensely depressed at the prospect

of this routine continuing indefinitely. Annika started wetting her bed when her father left, and still does occasionally; that obviously doesn't help.

Doreen is a woman of character. She is strong and courageous. She has faced despair, but she has not succumbed. She has been abandoned by a man who has not been back to see his children even once. Worse, she has been messed around in an intolerable, bureaucratic, incompetent manner by a social and judicial system which exemplifies everything that is wrong with English public life. It seems that not much has changed since Dickens was tilting at similar injustices 150 years ago.

CHAPTER SIX

POTENTIAL UNLIMITED

Dover

I set out through south-east London—along the Old Kent Road, through New Cross and up Blackheath Hill—the ancient route taken by pilgrims to Canterbury—on my way to Dover.

Now Dover had not been given good advance notices. Roland Castro, who divides his time between London and Deal, just up the road from Dover, told me: "Dover is horrid. A town without a soul." One of his assistants, Angela, who lives in Ashford, also nearby, said: "Dover is dismal and boring. Don't stay there one moment more than you have to."

I looked up Dover in a book by David W. Lloyd, *Historic Towns of South East England*, which I was to find invaluable. Lloyd's first sentence on Dover is blunt: "Dover is a sad and sorry town in a setting that is magnificent, both scenically and historically."

So I arrived without high expectations: and I was soon disposed to endorse everything I had been told. The first restaurant I came to, The Townall Fish and Steak Restaurant, was "Closed for Staff Holidays" which seemed surprising in mid-May. Then I walked up the main thoroughfare towards High Street: Beach Street, and then the pedestrianised Cannon Street and Biggin Street. They were well-nigh deserted—and this was a Saturday afternoon, a time when the shopping areas of most English towns are excessively busy. I counted no fewer than seventeen shops that were permanently shut—either boarded up without explanation, or with to let signs showing. This was dispiriting.

I wanted an overview of the town; I saw some steps leading up a steep grassy hill immediately to the west, and headed in that direction. When I reached them, they proved to be scruffy and weed-ridden. They led up to the "Western Heights", an extensive series of old battlements and ramparts in a superb situation high above the Western Docks. As I walked around, there were remarkably few people about. I came across a French family, an elderly lady jogger, a courting couple and a man walking his dog. Perhaps the local people avoid the area, given its squalid condition. It was disgracefully unkempt. Nasty, vicious-looking barbed wire protected the ramparts and the cliffs—possibly to save life and limb, but it need not have been so ugly—and there was not a seat or a bench in sight, even at the more obvious viewpoints. There was litter everywhere. The worst mess was in the car park near the back of St Martin's Battery: fast food detritus, a lot of old newspapers, a discarded girlie magazine, an old red sandal, stray bits of filthy clothing. There was not a litter bin in sight, though I am not sure it would have made much difference. A bird had evacuated spectacularly on one of the glass-covered signs explaining the history of the Western Heights. Somehow that seemed appropriate. On every available stone surface there were graffiti. Most of it was incomprehensible but on one of the old battery walls the message, in big red letters, was stark and to the point: PISS OFF.

Good advice, I thought, for the place was baneful and eerie. Far below, between the Prince of Wales Pier and the Admiralty Pier, was a purposeful and preferable scene, with cars, hovercraft, trains and ferries all neatly laid out.

Potential Unlimited

As I circumnavigated the Heights, I came across the most spectacular piece of rubbish yet; an old TV set, dumped by the track. I passed a shed with a huge mound of old tyres piled against it. It looked derelict but a notice said: Tip Top Repairs. The fabric of this entire area could do with some repairs, and fast.

All this might not matter so much, but for two considerations. First, the site is potentially breathtaking. It commands the gateway to England and it is replete with military and other historical associations. It provides wonderful views of Dover and its two great dock areas, of the Channel and—on clear days—of France. Secondly, tourists are actually exhorted to visit the Western Heights. I came across several notices urging me to "Explore the Western Heights".

After this, things could only get better. And they did. The next morning was gloriously sunny. I rose early and walked along the front. It is graced by a fine shallow crescent (1834-8) by Philip Hardwick, a crescent which includes the White Cliffs Hotel, where I was staying. Further along, towards the huge Eastern Docks complex, are two modern blocks of flats, which while less aesthetically pleasing, are by no means ugly. The White Cliffs, meanwhile, were gleaming in the sunshine. They looked pristine.

Then I came to the docks area, with Dover Castle looming high above. The A2 road from Canterbury goes through open country immediately beyond the castle, and sweeps down to the dock entrance in a splendid haughty curve—thus bypassing Dover, as if the town were not worth visiting, as if people simply wanted to get on their ferries as fast as possible, to get out of England as fast as possible. And no doubt many of them do.

Beneath the cliffs, by the side of the docks, a narrow path climbs under the concrete supports of the A2, and on upwards towards the high Langdon clifftops. Half way up this path, I encountered a strange scene.

A tall, bearded man was shouting animatedly and waving a knife around. An old couple were nodding nervously, looking most anxious to get on their way. They seized on my arrival as an opportunity to leave. The man turned to me and said: "Ah, you are being chased by the maidens." I look round and, sure enough, two girls were making their way up the path behind me. But they didn't linger; they rushed past in alarm when they saw this manic figure jumping around with his knife.

I had a good look at him. Very dark and weather-beaten, he was heavily bearded and sported an ancient, filthy baseball cap. I reckoned he was about fifty, but it was hard to tell. He looked like a demented Fidel Castro, down on his luck.

"What's your name?" I asked.

"Wally," he said. "Here in England, Wally. In Germany it was Fritz. It depends where I am."

We then had a long conversation. I was not taking notes but I wrote up what was said immediately afterwards, in Dover Castle, and the following is, I think, an accurate account of our encounter.

Wally was living in an improvised lean-to by the path. An old pram guarded the entrance. I asked if he had survived the winter there. Easy, he said. No problem. And indeed, he looked well. He told me he had been there since the previous summer, but he was always ready to move on, if need be.

All his possessions were in his pram. He had been in England since 1948, first doing a variety of work, then drifting round jobless in the Midlands, and then in Sussex and Kent. He had been in the Dover area for about six years.

I asked, gently, why he was waving his knife around. "I use it for my garden," he said. He needed a knife to cut down saplings, to protect the area around his lean-to. He also needed it to keep the area tidy. And indeed he had planted some flowers, which he showed me.

I asked how old he was. "Work it out," he said. "February 1925, I was born." I asked where he came from. "My mother was Russian," he said. "My father came from near Turkey, near the Black Sea. You know?" I tried: Georgia? Ukraine? Armenia? Bulgaria? Was he a Kurd? He said, very aggressively: "Bullshit. These are all number plates. Bullshit. These countries don't exist."

I changed the subject as diplomatically as possible. He must like England if he had stayed here since 1948. "England—hah!" he said. "I call it Ink-land. All paper, paperwork. All this bureau-bureaucracy. All this devil's invention, television."

At last, he laid down the knife. Then he put it in a pail beside the pram. "There are bad boys in England now," he said.

Evidently local youths had been coming up the cliffs to attack him. But he was too fast for them, he said. He could make things that saw them off, no matter how fast they thought they were. "A catapult?" He laughed and laughed, but said nothing.

His English had a pronounced East European accent, but he used the language with vigour. He told me it took him five years to learn it. Before he could speak English he felt he was more in—he searched for a word, then said, harmony—with the English people. I suggested the word empathy. He didn't know it. He said the English language was too good, too technical. It was too precise for real contact.

The conversation was becoming philosophical. At this point we were joined by an elderly lady puffing up the path. She seemed disposed to chat; the knife was now out of sight. Wally asked aggressively where she came from.

"Dover."

"And what do you call yourself?"

"A Dover shark."

And Wally clapped his hands and laughed loudly. I asked if she was a Dover shark because she ripped off tourists. She didn't object to this somewhat tasteless remark. "No," she said, "we're all called Dover sharks around here."

She pointed down to the great docks below and said she could remember when there was nothing there. "Nothing at all. Just peace and quiet."

I asked about the A2 curving in past the Castle, directly into the docks. Surely it kept a lot of potential business from the town? She agreed, but said that was the way Dover people wanted it. And Wally agreed vehemently. "You don't want traffic going this way, traffic going that way in the little town," he said.

Dear Country

The lady observed a departing ferry and said she didn't like the look of the modern ships. Too top-heavy, she thought. They looked dangerous. Wally disagreed. They had plenty of ballast down below, he insisted.

The lady took her leave. Wally asked where I came from. "Scotland," I said. He wanted to know why I was not small and aggressive, like a Scottish dog. "And you don't wear the skirt."

"Kilt," I said.

He asked if I played the pipes.

"No," I said, forbearing to add the famous line from a classic *Hancock's Half Hour*: We're not all Rob Roys.

He told me he had once heard the pipes played in Oxfordshire. A lament, it was. One of the most beautiful sounds he had ever heard.

As I said goodbye, he asked me to arrange for some books to be sent to him from Scotland. "Just send them down with one of your lorry drivers, and leave them with the police at the docks."

He said the police knew him and and got on well with him.

I hope they do, for when I reached the end of the path, at the entrance to the Langdon Cliffs site which is owned by the National Trust, I had a chat with the attendant. I told him of my encounter with the Russian tramp.

"He's not Russian, he's Polish," the man said. "And anyway, he's a menace. He has got to go."

I asked why, and was told that Wally had been cutting down trees at the back of the row of coastguards' houses, where this man lived. The trees were needed to protect the houses from the constant noise of traffic on the A2.

"He's got to go," the man repeated. "He can't keep cutting down trees." As I say, I hope Wally had some influential friends.

I then walked down the back road which led, over the A2, to Dover Castle. I took a little detour into the woods to see the Bleriot Memorial, a simple imprint of the shape of his plane on the exact spot where the aviator landed on 25 July 1909. Now it's surrounded by trees. There was no-one else around. It was very quiet, considering the proximity of the A2 and the busy docks.

I then walked up to the Castle, which is run by English Heritage and costs £3 to enter (more if you want to visit Hellfire Corner, but I decided to forego that pleasure). It is a huge, groomed complex, with the inevitable shop, restaurants, exhibition and a big car park. There are underground works, tunnels, towers, halls, a keep, a Roman lighthouse, a church, and much else. To explore it properly would have taken at least four hours.

I chose instead to walk round the perimeter. Unfortunately, there was no viewpoint at the obvious spot, immediately above the harbour. Here France is only seventeen miles away. Large fences protected the scrublands along the clifftop, with notices saying Keep Out.

After the carefully manicured lawns and the spacious formality of Dover Castle, it was pleasant to stroll downhill to the Dover Transport Museum, where informality is the rule.

A wonderful clutter of old cars, buses, fire engines and other vehicles; a cornucopia of models, timetables, posters and other transport memorabilia. Outside there was a miniature train ride for the kids. By it, two old men were carefully restoring a 1950s lorry.

This is our more recent—and in a sense our more meaningful—heritage, being lovingly tended by amateurs. The museum is run as a hobby by enthusiasts, in premises leased by the Folkestone and District Water Company. But, as I was told by the man who gave me my ticket, only until the end of 1991.

I asked if they had new premises available. "We have a few options available, but we need help." Were the Council helping? "They say they want to. I hope they will." And so do I. There was a pleasant feel to this museum: something intimate and idiosyncratic. The ticket cost £1. The Dover Castle ticket, at £3, offered, to be fair, more than three times more to look at. But the transport museum enjoyed what so much of the heritage industry cannot provide—a sense of individuality and personality.

I walked down the hill through Dover's upmarket district (not a designation devised by some yuppie estate agent, but a reference to the fact that the town's second, alternative, market used to be held here, just beyond the town bounds). As I walked, I looked along the town, at ease and comfortable in its cleft. By far the most prominent building, simply because of its garish red colour, was the B&Q Superstore. It is the same in many English towns.

Various people in Dover had told me that the town attracted few residential tourists, basically because there was nothing to do. A serious effort to counter this had just been opened, days earlier, in the shape of the "White Cliffs Experience", billed brashly as "the ultra-modern visitor centre which includes dramatic displays on the theme of England's turbulent history".

I went to have a look, but there was a long queue, consisting mainly of French tourists. Contrary to the characteristics ascribed by (English) folk wisdom, they were queueing in a most orderly and patient manner.

I decided I could not be bothered waiting. Also, it was a glorious day, by now into its latter stages, and I wanted to enjoy what remained of it. I walked along Snargate Street to the Western Docks, which I had viewed, in bilious mood, the evening before from the Western Heights.

Snargate Street was a delight. It had the feel of a street leading to a genuine port, unlike Marine Parade which leads to the modern Eastern Docks. Snargate Street is lined with ships' chandlers, marine suppliers, cafés offering all-day breakfasts and gargantuan fry-ups, angling shops selling tackle, lug and other fresh bait. There are furtive back yards and shifty-looking import businesses. Trucks lethargically ground past, without the purpose of the lorries at the eastern end. The grinding and clanking of a train, slowly making its way out to the far docks, was interrupted by the brutally loud roar of a hovercraft setting off (a sound which punctuates every activity in daytime Dover). I walked on and came eventually to the magnificent old Marine Station, towards the end of the great pier. Here there was a shop and a buffet, both open, and a vast, clean waiting area. Two trains were standing at platforms, but the place was virtually deserted and the mood was like that of a cathedral just before evensong, as the western sun slanted in through the vaulted glass roof. I walked on and on, surprised that I could get this far without being challenged—or indeed venturing anywhere that, apparently, I should not be—and looked round the huge open spaces and the Admiralty pier end, which stretches 1,300 yards out into the Channel. There was not a soul in sight, although there was much activity across the water on the other side of the western harbour, at the hoverport.

I returned to the station as an eight-coach train was preparing to leave for Victoria. I counted sixteen passengers, or two for each coach, though I may have missed one or two. It clanked slowly out of the station, like an emissary for a lost way of life.

Dover is by far the busiest passenger port in Europe. Obviously most of these passengers use the Eastern Docks. The Western Docks, possibly for that very reason, had more appeal, and certainly more charm and character.

My first impression of Dover had been bad, even atrocious, but by the time I left I had grown to like the place. Everybody I met in the town was helpful and friendly.

Dover is an enigma. It has faced a longstanding dilemma. At present it is the least attractive of the Cinque Ports (or so I am told; I have not visited them all) but then it has a great pressing workaday function that the others lack.

It is where so many people bid farewell to England, or set foot on it for the first time. Its physical situation is stupendous. Its historical associations are legion. It was just off Dover that the defeat of the Spanish Armada started in earnest; it was here that Charles II landed at the Restoration in 1660.

Dover is like a mantra running through Shakespeare's greatest play, *King Lear*. Lord Byron spent his last bittersweet days in England here, before he fled abroad, pursued by creditors. And so I could go on . . .

And yet Dover has had a grievously bad press. "The cracked white cups of Dover tea shops" I had been told. "The shabby off-white cliffs" was another jeer.

Dear Country

So: Should Dover try to make all these millions of passers-through linger? Should it try to beguile them? Perhaps the Channel Tunnel, that behemoth taking shape down the road, will force such decisions on it. Soon, Dover will no longer be able to make a good living simply by shunting the incomers and outgoers through, and enjoying its own sluggish life in the cleft between the most famous cliffs in all the world. Soon, it will have to discover its full potential. I wish it well: its potential is endless.

CHAPTER SEVEN

EXTINGUISHED RESORT

Brighton—Hove

Brighton and Hove sit uneasily beside each other on the most celebrated stretch of Sussex coastline. Brighton is England's greatest seaside resort: Hove, a relative newcomer, consoles itself with its avoidance of such Brighton characteristics as vulgarity and tattiness. Notices abound in Hove, informing you that it is "separate and very different from Brighton".

Brighton did not invent the dirty weekend, but succeeded, as it were, in patenting that institution as its own. It is at once downmarket and prosperous. It is one of the wealthiest towns in England, yet it has a large population of down-and-outs. In some ways its disparities and contradictions mirror those of London, and Brighton has for long been known as London by the sea. It has a large gay population, a serious drugs problem, and a reputation for sporadic and pointless violence. Brighton has featured in innumerable novels and films, from Graham Greene's *Brighton Rock* to Neil Jordan's *Mona Lisa*: it is often portrayed as unpleasant and seedy. For all that, it possesses abundant vitality and a raffish kind of style. Hove seems atrophied beside it.

Hove's seafront has manicured lawns, and no shops or fish and chip cafés or other such excrescences. It has, of course, no pier. Brighton, on the other hand, has the magnificent Palace Pier (entry free and, even better, deck chairs free) which, lit up at night, looks quite beautiful, even ethereal. Brighton also has the West Pier, now derelict and in urgent need of demolition (a sad reminder, for me, of Skegness).

Hove lacks a cinema or a theatre. Its main shops and a few of its dreary pubs are to be found in Church Street, a long road parallel to the esplanade which features among other buildings an ugly new town hall and an interesting church, superbly renovated by George Baseri. Unfortunately, this church is adjacent to a large gasworks, which dominates a considerable stretch of the street.

There is something ludicrous about Hove's efforts to emphasise its distinction from Brighton. The notices mentioned earlier emphasise that it's "A distinguished resort with a more peaceful atmosphere than Brighton". When it started promoting itself as "a distinguished resort" the local graffiti merchants had a field day, defacing the signs to read either "a last resort" or, more wittily and neatly, "an extinguished resort".

Hove does possess some fine terraces and crescents, but it has nothing to compare with Kemp Town (named after the tragic MP, T. R. Kemp) at the eastern (non-Hove) end of Brighton, where Lewes Square and Sussex Square comprise an undoubted masterpiece.

The dividing line between Brighton and Hove consists of Waterloo Street, a narrow, scruffy street leading down to the front. It has a variety of ethnic restaurants, a pub, a shut-up church and a plethora of B&Bs. More Brighton than Hove, I'd say.

I decided to take the Portsmouth bus from Hove along the coast to Felpham, which is of interest because it was here that William Blake conceived and started the great sequence of poems *Milton*. (The famous lines of Jerusalem are from the preface.) The fare was £3.60, not bad for a journey taking two hours forty minutes, there and back. The timetable said that this Southdown Coastliner service was financially supported by West Sussex Council.

The double-decker bus had only a handful of passengers when I boarded it at Hove; there were even fewer on the return journey. From my seat on the upper deck I had a good view of the coastal towns we passed through: Shoreham, Lancing, Worthing and Littlehampton. Shoreham was a surprise: a big port, more industrialised than I had expected, and no doubt rather too industrialised for its neighbour Hove. To the right of Lancing, inland, I could see Lancing College, where Evelyn Waugh was so unhappy, and where Henry Thorold laboured as a housemaster. Its huge chapel loomed disproportionately above the gentle green slopes.

As we left Worthing, passing row after row of neat villas and bungalows, I began to marvel at the state of the gardens. They were all immaculate, colourful, inordinately, excessively tidy. I began to look for a mess. Surely West Worthing must allow at least one maverick anti-gardener? Eventually, after several minutes, I gave up looking for an untidy garden. By this time we were in Littlehampton, and nearing Felpham, which was reached by one of the rare stretches of road traversing open country. It was a relief to get away from the ribbons of neat maisonettes and bungalows. Was this Blake's "green and pleasant land"? From upstairs on the bus it looked pleasant enough, and certainly very green.

I got off at the Southdowns pub and asked the first person I met, a woman walking her dog, for directions to Blake's cottage. "At last a place I know," she said with a laugh. But the way was complicated. She directed me to the post office, where I could get further directions. From the post office, it was very near: a thatched cottage, side on to Blakes Road, only 100 yards or so from the sea. A notice in a window said: *Not On View. Private.*

As far as I could make out, through the thick fence, there was an extraordinarily beautiful garden.

Blake, a Londoner through and through, was invited to Felpham by the local squire, a pretentious buffoon called Hayley, a man of considerable literary pretentions. At first Blake was happy in Felpham, but soon he began to fret.

He found the cottage damp. As the *Dictionary of National Biography* puts it: "It was not to be expected that he could long continue to breathe freely in the atmosphere of elegant triviality and shallow sentiment which surrounded the literary squire."

Eventually Blake returned to London after one of the more farcical episodes in English literary history. A drunken soldier entered the cottage garden. Blake understandably evicted him and was promptly charged with sedition. He was duly acquitted at Chichester; but he had had enough of Sussex. He was to write later:

> *The Sussex men are noted fools*
> *and weak is their brain-pan.*

I wondered what would have happened if, in all sobriety, I had ventured into the cottage garden, and been thrown out by the present owner.

The Rev. Henry Thorold had told me that Felpham was "just a tedious suburb of Bognor", but I found it a serene and pleasant place. It was well endowed with five pubs (there may be even more, but I passed five on my walk to the cottage). I went into The Fox, for a couple of pints of Ruddles County. Apart from the woman behind the bar, I must have been the only person under seventy. The other customers were having an animated conversation about today's youth. Most of those taking part—six or seven—were disposed to be generous: the view was that there were always a few bad ones, and that this generation had neither more nor less than any other. But one old dear insisted that most of today's youngsters were bad, and obsessed by money. "They need it for their drugs," she kept saying.

And maybe she had a point. The Drugs Advice and Information Service reckons that it can be easier for youngsters to buy drugs than cigarettes in the Brighton area, and that there are about 2,000 young people in West Sussex regularly using LSD and Ecstasy.

I returned to Hove—another pleasant bus journey—and in the evening I made my way to Queen's Park, past the centre of Brighton, towards Kemp Town. Here I was to see an open-air production of *Romeo and Juliet* by the Reaction Theatre Company, which is geared to giving young actors early professional experience.

The company charged £4 for a ticket. The audience was invited to sit on grass in a natural amphitheatre at a corner of the park. You could easily see and hear from beyond the railings, but only five or six cheapskates took advantage of this. As 7.30 approached I reckoned there were about 400 people in the audience. They were predominantly young, although there were a few oldies, and there were quite a few children, and one baby. There were hardly any middle-aged people such as myself. I felt quite bereft as I had brought no drink, food or sweets, though a family beside me kindly offered me some wine. There was a great deal of guzzling from hampers, and drinking of wine. Many thermos flasks were in evidence, but nothing as vulgar as a beer can—until at last I saw a red-sweatered young man surreptitiously swigging lager. Champagne corks were still popping as a little string band started playing to signify the start of the performance. There was a certain amount of eating, drinking and chatting through the show, but for the most part the members of the audience were rapt and so they should have been, for this was a very lively, enthusiastic performance. The company made excellent use of the space, and all the trees, and leapt in and out of the audience when the mood took them. There were some vigorous fight sequences. It was all very energetic and wholehearted, and devoid of any preciousness or pomposity.

The odd line was lost and there were occasional noises off. First these came from children playing in the nearby playground. There were also traffic sounds. One car hooted rudely and revved aggressively, but others appeared to slow down and steal past as quietly as possible. Then some kids (aged about eleven or twelve) appeared and threw clods of earth into the audience from the rear, but they were chased away amid laughter rather than anger. It slowly grew darker, and much colder. Some people did grow restless, but most maintained their attention to the end. The baby was asleep. It was a very English affair, somehow innocent, sylvan and eccentric, all at once.

The next morning I drove up to the Stanner Park campus of the University of Sussex, designed by Sir Basil Spence in the 1960s. Here I was to meet a friend, Graham Walker, who teaches history at the university, and two of his colleagues—Andy Medhurst (Media Studies) and Lindsay Smith (Eng. Lit.). Together they represented a cross-section of the younger arts lecturers. Graham had warned me that the arts car parks would be full, and had advised me to park in the science area, where there would be plenty of space: he turned out to be absolutely right. (I wonder what that says about higher education in Sussex.)

Over lunch at the Gardner Centre we discussed many topics. I described my bus trip of the previous day, and then confessed that that had been an exception: I was travelling almost everywhere by car. I felt guilty about not using public transport more on my journey. "Don't worry about that. It would take you at least three years to get round England if you used public transport," said Andy. "And even then you wouldn't manage to get to half the places."

Andy, who does not have a car, recalled that he used to live in Norwich: "It was very easy to get to London. But you simply weren't supposed to go anywhere else by public transport. That was almost impossible."

We then talked about the current crop of students. Graham, a rigorous Scot who is appalled by the inability of some of his students to write grammatical English, and who is teasingly described by his colleagues as "a pedagogic fascist", said that at Sussex, and other universities, students had a tendency to scrutinise what they were taught, and why they were taught it.

That was not necessarily a bad thing, but sometimes students shopped around too much, so that they ended up learning a bit of this, a bit of that; a bit from this course, a bit from that course. He said he did not want to sound old-fashioned but he felt that students should value the worth of education, of learning, for its own sake rather more than they did.

I asked about the science car parks. All three said that Sussex was very much an arts-oriented university; they felt that there was considerable difficulty in getting intelligent school-leavers to study science, because science only became interesting after the undergraduate level. Science students were allowed much less self-expression than arts students.

When we turned to the state of England, Andy was adamant that no self-respecting liberal intellectual could possibly say: "I'm proud to be English." (Here was an uncanny echo of what George Orwell had written exactly fifty years earlier: "England is perhaps the only great country whose intellectuals are ashamed of their own nationality.")

It simply was not progressive, he said, to endorse any of the values that were commonly perceived to be English. He mentioned here the imperialistic legacy, which he reckoned to be more potent that was often allowed. An endorsement of English values could be left to the tabloid press, or the monarchy.

Nonetheless, Andy avowed that culturally he was quite proud of England. It was the notion of a cohesive England rolling smoothly along that terrified him; it would be like living permanently in a heritage centre—or living in Lincolnshire. (This last was specifically for my benefit—I had been describing my travels round Lincolnshire.) Andy went on to suggest that most received notions of England were essentially rural. He enjoyed looking round English villages as much as anyone else—but only as a holiday from real life.

Lindsay felt that to some extent English values, over the years, had been represented by a distorted interpretation of English literature, and Shakespeare in particular. I said that surely nobody could regard Shakespeare himself as a glib, unthinking chauvinist. I cited the famous John of Gaunt speech from *Richard II*, which is so often quoted out of context as a simplistic celebration of England: "This royal throne of kings, this sceptred isle/ this earth of majesty, this seat of Mars/ this other Eden, demi-paradise. . ." and so on. But this great passage concludes:

"This land of such dear souls, this dear dear land/ Dear for her reputation through the world,/ Is now leased out—I die pronouncing it—/ Like to a tenement or pelting farm./ England, bound in with the triumphant sea,/ Whose rocky shore beats back the envious siege/ Of watery Neptune, is now bound in with shame,/ With inky blots and rotten parchment bonds./ That England, that was wont to conquer others,/ Hath made a shameful conquest of itself." Thus a passage that is actually expressing disgust about the condition of England is turned into a parody of patriotism; thus Shakespeare is in effect traduced for the purposes of bombastic or sentimental glorification of England.

Lindsay conceded the point, but what concerned her was not the actual text of Shakespeare's plays but what she termed "Bardolatry, the Stratford industry". I suggested that the academic study of English literature could help to temper this sort of thing. After all, Oxford University had just appointed as its Warton Professor of English Literature Terry Eagleton, for long the marxist *enfant terrible* of lit. crit. At this Andy said with enormous, jovial cynicism: "Yes, but Prince Charles making a speech invoking Shakespeare still means a great deal to a lot of English people. Maybe it shouldn't, but it does. Terry Eagleton giving a lecture about Shakespeare is, unfortunately, hardly in the same league. Anyway," he added, feeling that the conversation was becoming obscure, "go into Brighton, go into the real world, and ask about Shakespeare—and a lot of people wouldn't know who he was, unless they were students—and a lot of them wouldn't know either."

We then talked about London. I reminded Graham that when he'd lived and worked in the capital he had nurtured an almost apocalyptic vision of London as a great out-of-control international city, whose links with the rest of England were becoming increasingly tenuous.

He said that he had modified that view a little, perhaps just because he was no longer living in the capital. Andy said that in any discussion of modern London, the key had to be the abolition of the GLC. It was impossible to exaggerate what a disaster that had been, and it was still bitterly resented. Transport was obviously a huge problem in London—yet there was no planning, strategic body to organise it.

Lindsay, who comes from Nottingham, said there was an assumption in London and the south-east that the Midlands did not exist; they were just "part of the North". England was being pulled, intellectually and culturally, to the south. As for London, most people living there could not really appreciate it. As a visitor, she found it vibrant; but when she had lived there, she—and every other young person of her means—had had to live so far out from the centre that it was not really London at all.

I then discussed with Lindsay the literary heritage industry. I said I did not understand why some writers, rooted in a particular locality, were ignored, whereas others were exploited to the point of overkill. I cited Tennyson in Lincolnshire—the greatest Victorian poet, in many ways the supreme poet of the English landscape, who spent his entire early life in the Lincolnshire Wolds, and wrote so well about them. But, interjected Lindsay, Tennyson was simply not fashionable. Students were just not interested in him.

And that, I suppose, begs some questions. How do students determine who and what interests them? And a different, but perhaps related point: who decides to start a "Tennyson Trail", or whatever? Is it by popular demand; or is it because of the entrepreneurial zeal of a local tourist officer, or the enthusiasm of a local literateur? Lindsay mentioned John Clare, one of the most interesting of England's poets. There is a clear, well-defined Clare country (in the vicinity of Peterborough) but of a Clare industry, there is no sign whatsoever.

(Maybe that is just as well. But literary tourism need not be crass or exploitative or debasing. When I was in Dorset I was quite impressed by the Hardy industry. It was intensive, but it was also dignified and thoughtful. England is a supremely literary country, with a literature of unparalleled fecundity; but it certainly picks and chooses which of its many great authors it wants to celebrate. Fashion is fickle, of course; but I do not understand why Hardy should be so popular, Tennyson so unpopular.)

All this is, of course, another digression. Talking to Andy, who had an easy, charming scepticism, and to Lindsay, who was altogether more ardent, more intense, I was struck by how difficult, if not impossible, it is for intelligent young English people to isolate what it is that they identify with in their country—what symbolises their nationhood for them. In other words, they find it easy to focus on what they dislike about England; much less easy to say what England means to them.

Before I left Brighton and Hove, I decided to hire a bike, remembering my felicitous experience in Cambridge. I inquired at Hove's Tourist Information Centre, and they gave me two addresses (both in Brighton, needless to say).

The first was Harman Hire, near the station. The man there was not helpful. He asked me for a £50 deposit, though I only wanted the bike for a few hours. But fair enough; and it was also fair enough to ask for proof of identity. I had two credit cards and a British Telecom charge card.

"Inadequate," he said.

"Why?" I asked.

"Don't have your home address or photograph on them."

I said I was even prepared to raise the deposit.

"No go," he said. "The deposit is for any damage you might do to the bike. The identification is in case you steal it. Our bikes are very expensive, good quality. Our insurers insist on proper identification."

This was all very different from Geoff's at Cambridge. I left Harman Hire without a bike and convinced that I looked like a bicycle thief. Nonetheless, I walked down to the other hire shop, Sunrise Cycle Hire. This turned out to be just a hut in front of the derelict West Pier. The man there was friendly;

indeed he could not have been more affable. He wanted £4 for the hire. There was no deposit. He did ask for some identity; I offered a credit card and he said that was fine.

It was a nice bike, an old-fashioned Pashley. I cycled along the front to Shoreham. West Hove soon gives way to Shoreham Harbour, which is a busy if unsightly place, full of people working . (Hove seemed to be full of people not working, complaining about people not working.)

Shoreham, incidentally, is a town which takes the vogue for ecology more seriously than most. The biggest recycling experiment in Europe (or so they claim) is taking place there. Rubbish is collected twice over, recyclable material being put out in separate containers.

I returned round the back of Hove, and across to the hilly part of Brighton, between the Pavilion and Kemp Town. I had not realised just how steep parts of Brighton are; you soon get to know the ups and downs of a place on a bike. Then I cycled back along the front, past the Brighton Centre, which can accommodate more than 5,000 conference delegates; how far-sighted the civic leaders were to plan it fifteen years ago. It cost £9m but it has proved a fine investment, even if it is an eyesore. And past the Grand Hotel, where the IRA almost murdered half the Cabinet in 1984; the building was still scarred down its western flank, where reconstruction work was continuing.

I returned the bike to the pleasant man at Sunrise Hire, and had a last look back at what—for me—is Brighton's greatest glory: not the Pavilion, not even Kemp Town, but the Palace Pier. Its centenary is due in 1999. I hope it is celebrated with suitably vulgar *éclat*. Of course, the citizens of Hove will be disdainful, no matter what form the celebrations take.

CHAPTER EIGHT

HEAVY FARE AND HEAVY AIR

Dorset—Somerset—Wiltshire

I drove past Bournemouth—through pine woods, thinking of Henry Thorold and Sir John Betjeman and Woodhall Spa—towards Chideock, the little village that had produced the magnificent parish map I'd seen in Sue Clifford's office.

Chideock is in Dorset, very much an up-and-down county; there are no really high hills, but the dips are steep, and many of the villages are settled claustrophobically in low hollows. Chideock is like this.

The guiding force behind the Chideock parish map project, Kate Geraghty, does not live in Chideock itself, but in nearby Seatown, which is not a town, indeed it is hardly even a hamlet, though it is by the sea. I turned off at Chideock, which turned out to be a lovely village full of thatched cottages, and drove down Duck Road, a narrow lane with high hedges on either side, towards the sea. Kate lives in a splendid house above the Anchor Inn at the road end. She told me the history of the map.

It started with a couple of local people reading the Common Ground publications about parish maps. An open meeting was held in Chideock Village Hall on 6 July 1988, when twenty-six people said they were interested in producing a map. Of these, fourteen proceeded to become actively involved.

The mappers met monthly. A questionnaire was placed in the village shops. A tea was held in the hall in March 1989; all the villagers were invited to bring old photographs and other memorabilia. The resultant information was given to a local artist, Gillian Moores, who had agreed to draw the map.

Through the interest generated at this stage, the New Chideock Society was formed in July 1989, at a meeting in the hall attended by over 100 people. (The population of Chideock is just over 600.) The finished map was unveiled on 26 May 1990. All the village shops and the garage had copies for sale; over 400 were sold on the first day. The original map is still on display in the village hall.

It is an artefact of genuine beauty and originality, which manages to convey a great deal of information about Chideock's past and present while appearing essentially decorative rather than didactic. The actual map is in the form of a bird's eye view of the village and its environs; quirky "lozenges" with incidental details are featured along the top, and historical notes balance these along the bottom.

The map was created by both old and new residents. This is an important point, for all over England villages tend to be divided between longstanding residents and incomers, who can appear pushy and officious. Kate reckoned that the project did bring the village community together as never before. As well as the refounding of the Chideock Society, its most significant offshoot, the tradition of village fêtes was revived.

But she remained cautious: "There is still in Chideock, and I think this is probably true of most villages in Dorset, Devon and Somerset, a real division between the people who were born and brought up in the village, and the newer residents. The people who have been in the village for years and years, often for generations, can easily resent the newcomers, who may well be quite old retired folk, but who tend to want to make their mark. The people who have been born here sometimes take no part in the community whatsoever, yet they sneer at those they call the 'Surreyites'."

Such tensions could arise over something as simple as thatched roofing, which while undoubtedly picturesque, can be full of vermin. It tends to be the incomers who want to preserve such things, while the longstanding residents want to put in modern roofing, to concrete over old paths, and so on. Yet it is often these longstanding residents who have encouraged and enabled the incomers to move in, through selling some of their land.

Kate says that she is not yet accepted as a local, although she has been a resident for sixteen years. "The co-operation when we produced the map was terrific. Now the momentum is definitely slipping away somewhat."

Kate is a delightful, vivacious, spirited woman, a little larger than life: the sort that any community needs to drive it on, but also the type whom the more sluggish members of a bucolic community are likely to resent. A professional actress and theatrical director—her stage name is Kate Lansbury—she founded, with Belinda Low, the Somerset and Dorset Theatre Company in 1985. Since then they have put on twelve shows and toured throughout the two far-flung counties. She buzzes round this rather enervated countryside, bringing a little zip and zest, a little colour and fresh air.

I moved on west into Devon to visit the famous donkey sanctuary near Sidmouth. Started by Mrs E. D. Svendsen in 1969, it has grown steadily to the extent that it is now a complex of five farms, from which inspectors sally forth to keep an eye on the welfare of donkeys up and down the entire UK. About eight donkeys a week are taken into care. Mrs Svendsen recently expanded her concern—the average life of a donkey abroad is apparently only eleven years, whereas in England it is thirty-seven years. She therefore founded the International Donkey Protection Trust which aims to improve conditions for donkeys throughout the world.

Mrs Svendsen and the sanctuary received much attention a few years ago when, with the much trumpeted assistance of the tabloid press, and the *Daily Star* in particular, they managed to rescue the donkey now known as Blackie Star from the infamous Villanueva de la Vera fiesta in Spain. (The egregious custom was for the fattest man in town to be placed on a donkey, which was then hauled through the streets by fifty strong men. Drunken villagers were encouraged to taunt and attack the animal during this so-called celebration. This was such an obviously barbaric ritual that Mrs Svendsen's high-profile intervention was a considerable public relations coup.)

The sanctuary is open every day of the year. I found it a pleasant and well-organised place, for the most part devoid of the sentimentality, eccentricity and coyness I had been expecting.

Donkeys of every shape and size were obviously being well looked after. I watched a video display, but, in common with several other people, had to leave because one woman was guffawing so loudly—one donkey, Timothy, whose ears had been slashed by vandals (English, not Spanish) before it was taken to the sanctuary, raised its foot to "shake hands" with some old buffer. This sequence seemed to me silly rather than comic, but the lady was laughing so uproariously that she managed to clear the room.

An agreeable place, then, and a living endorsement of the celebrated kindness of the English to animals. But the obvious niggle must be whether all this energy and effort could not be better directed towards helping humans in distress rather than donkeys.

From the sanctuary I meandered down to Sidmouth, which was—well, very different from Skegness. A soporific little resort, it boasts an elected councillor, Stuart Hughes, who stood as the candidate of the Raving Loony Green Giant Party (not to be confused with the slightly different loony party of Lord Sutch, the parliamentary by-election specialist). Mr Hughes has been described as England's most powerful loony. Sidmouth also boasts an exquisite cricket ground, Fort Field, with the sea on one side; it is also flanked by hotels, by a gracious, gleaming terrace of white houses, and its own little thatched pavilion.

People—most of them aged—were promenading round the town in a measured way. The pace here seemed slow, very slow; the weather was hazy and it added to the dozy feel of the place. All over this part of England I felt a drowsiness, a heaviness verging on the comatose.

I stayed that night, and the next night, at Chedington Court. Chedington is a tiny village just off Winyard's Gap near Beaminster, in North Dorset; Chedington Court is a hotel, though the actual word is not used. Normally, I regard that as a bad sign: England is becoming full of small, country house hotels whose owners seem ashamed of their commercial status. Indeed, some of these establishments appear to be run not so much as overtly commercial ventures, but rather as discreet enterprises enabling their owners to live in the style to which they are not accustomed—in other words, as landed gentlefolk. As for that necessary evil, the guests, they can be made to feel like awkward, unwanted intruders.

This, happily, was not the case at Chedington Court, which soon won me over. The owners, Philip and Hilary Chapman, were self-effacing, Mrs Chapman to the point of invisibility (she did all the cooking). Mr Chapman seemed shy; he went round his guests asking gently if everything was all right, but he did not linger for strained or stiff conversations.

The house, built in 1840, is delightful, but the real glory of Chedington Court is its large garden, in which traditionally-tended terraces give way to steeper, wilder slopes. These ten acres afford spectacular views across North Dorset (on clear days you can also see into Somerset and Devon) in the direction of Syme's Hill, and the village of South Perrott.

When I first walked through these lovely grounds a fire was burning in a field far below (the hotel is 600 feet above sea level) and the flash of orange was the only garish note in a restrained rhapsody of dark green. The English country was looking at its most mature and rich. A train clattered through the valley, past Crewkerne Station; it sounded very close, yet the line was at least three miles away. Otherwise, all was still and quiet.

The next day was a Saturday. I drove carefully round the

Dorset villages—the roads tended to be narrow and twisty—half-enjoying, half-resenting the air of introversion and stickiness. Clotted cream teas were on sale everywhere, even in the morning; heavy fare to match the heavy air. It was not a sunny day, but an oppressive one; the air seemed to press in. The high hedges along the lanes and the muggy villages squatting in their hollows made Dorset seem closed in and stuffy. I felt constricted.

Then, in a long irregular village called Loders, I came across a fair. It was being held in a small green at the back of the Church of England primary school. Children were dancing round a maypole—a white pole which was held steady by two young boys. At its top was a garland of flowers. Green, yellow, blue and red ribbons were hanging from the pole; groups of three children clutched them and danced, or rather skipped round and round, twining their ribbons round the pole. When the tape-recorded music stopped, they turned and skipped in the opposite direction, thus unwinding their ribbons.

(Later I learned a little about Maypole dancing. In 1583, an Elizabethan commentator had noted that when the maidens went to the woods to cut hawthorn to deck the maypoles, scarcely a third returned in the same condition. It was an English custom to stay in the woods all night to bring in the month of May; not surprisingly, the Puritans disliked it, and eventually Oliver Cromwell banned maypoles altogether. The modern, prettified, anaesthetised ritual, in which children wind ribbons round a comparatively small pole—as at Loders—was apparently intoduced to England by John Ruskin just over a century ago.)

The dancers at Loders were ringed by a great crush of admiring parents, many of them with cameras, and other villagers. There were old folk, middle-aged folk, men and women in their twenties and thirties, and of course children; but no teenagers, so far as I could see.

I was surprised to see so many men present, because this was Cup Final afternoon, and I had just heard on my car radio a commentator bombastically announcing that there were many cup finals the world over, but there was only one true cup final—*and this was it*. Most of England would be listening or watching as Tottenham Hotspur played Nottingham Forest at Wembley.

Well, most of Loders was certainly not listening or watching. The innocent pastoral scene could not have contrasted more pointedly with the frantic hype I returned to when I got back into my car. All the talk was of Paul Gascoigne of Tottenham Hotspur. It had been Gazza's year. The most famous tears ever shed by an Englishman had been shed by Gazza at the World Cup eleven months earlier. Since then Gazza had become established as the most written about and talked about sportsman in England, the most famous Englishman, in fact. Spurs had to send him off to a health farm for a week to remove him from his circus of admirers and media hangers-on.

This callow, wayward, likeable Geordie dominated the press—quality as well as tabloid—during my time in England. And this Cup Final day was to be the climax, the magnificent apogee of Gazza's annus mirabilis, the triumphant zenith of months of Gazzamatazz.

Well, despite, or perhaps because of, the hysterical build-up to Gazza's Cup Final, his personal final lasted a mere seventeen minutes. During that time his contribution was wholly negative; he committed two bad fouls. The second led to his team, Spurs, going a goal down, for from the free kick he conceded, the captain of Forest, Stuart Pearce, scored directly. Worse, Gazza had seriously injured his knee in perpetrating the foul. He was carried off.

I was listening to all this drama—I can't avoid the word—as I drove through leafy Dorset. The commentators did not quite know how to react to Gazza's demise; he had deserved it in a sense, but now the final was bereft of its major player, *Hamlet* without the Prince. Was it a harsh irony, or even rough justice? I suspect there was some confusion, and maybe even a little guilt; the media had built up Gazza so much that his manic start to the game was to some extent their fault. Yet there was also a temptation to turn on the fallen hero, the erstwhile demigod. Anyway, there was something surreal about moving gently through sleepy, bucolic England listening to the turbulence and hysteria being relayed from Wembley. It was another variation on the two nations theme.

Finding it too claustrophobic inland, I headed south, towards the sea. At another long, straggling village, Abbotsbury—featuring many thatched cottages on pavements raised above the road—a cricket match was taking place: Abbotsbury Seconds (it seemed remarkable that such a modest village could sustain two cricket teams) against Old Blandfordians. The players were immaculately kitted out in impeccable white. The game was being played with calm, almost languorous, dignity; so different from the frenzy of Wembley.

High above, on a hilltop, stood the fifteenth-century St Catherine's Chapel; a few hundred yards away was the sea. The bells in the parish church were ringing; on the main street the blacksmith's door was open, affording a view of flame and anvil as a horse was shod. The scene was placid and rustic.

I returned to the car: more excitement. Spurs had equalised. Gazza was almost forgotten. Then in extra time, Spurs went ahead, and Gazza was forgotten. (Not, however, for long. The *knee* became the focus of England's attention. Daily, even hourly reports, were dispatched from the superstar's private hospital in Marylebone. His transfer to the Italian club Lazio was off, then it was back on, then it was off again. The very future of Spurs, in deep financial trouble, depended on the deal. This was a new subplot in the continuing soap opera. Italian media men, apparently sharp-suited beside the English scruffs, thronged the streets outside the hospital, desperate for the latest bulletin. They were joined by well-wishers, groupies, hangers-on, pubescent and sub-pubescent admirers of the great man, even the odd football fan. How ingenuous to think that a mere injury could terminate, or even suspend, England's obsession with Gazza.)

The next day, I continued my journey, now heading north into Somerset. I visited East Coker, which inspired the second of T. S. Eliot's *Four Quartets*. It is a bigger and less lonely place than Little Gidding—and that applies to the church, St Michael's, as well as the village.

Andrew Eliot, the poet's ancestor, who emigrated to America in 1660, was baptised in the church in 1627. The poet visited East Coker, just once, in 1937; and it is not known when he decided that he wanted to be buried there. But in the 1950s he made arrangements for his ashes to be buried in the north-west corner of the church, where a simple plaque asks the beholder to pray for the repose of his soul. He was buried on Easter Sunday, 1965, and since then many thousands of tourists have visited the church. I don't know how many of them have also visited Little Gidding, but that would seem to me a more fitting destination for a literary pilgrimage.

On the Sunday I visited East Coker, there was far more activity at the "antiques fayre" in the very modern village hall, where the large car park was full to overflowing, than at the church—though, to be fair, the morning service had just finished. Soon the only person left in the church was a lady tending to the flowers; she told me that East Coker was an exceptionally happy community, though the population had more than doubled in her lifetime.

My next destination was Glastonbury, which is the focus of more myths and legends than any other town in England. It is a reputed meeting point of leylines (supposedly dead straight prehistoric tracks) and a centre of "earth energy". The ground evidently resonates, and people have levitated. Strange lights have been spotted hovering in the night sky.

Glastonbury's mystique is a mixed blessing; it has become a cynosure for eccentrics and hippies from all over the world. If you so desire, you can learn about witchcraft here, or receive "alternative therapy". Not all of the visitors are welcome in the town, which is for the most part a workaday, even prosaic, place. There was little evidence of anything unusual when I was there. I did find some places in England which had a numinous quality: Little Gidding and Bag Enderby, for example. But not Glastonbury.

The present town was originally an island, rising from a vast lake. It is reckoned to have been founded by Christ's uncle, St Joseph of Arimathea, who arrived, with a band of disciples, one Christmas morning. The story goes that he stuck his staff into the ground; it sprouted and flowered, which he took to be a sign that this was a propitious place, and that his wanderings should cease. Joseph is also said to have brought the Holy Grail to Glastonbury.

Thus Glastonbury is a very special place for English Christians, although some of the pilgrims who are drawn to it insist that it had a spiritual significance long before Christianity. Glastonbury has a further legendary claim: that it is the place where King Arthur and Queen Guinevere are buried.

These are all legends; what is fact is that in 1685 there was a brutal battle between the Duke of Monmouth's rebels and royal troops at nearby Westonzoyland. The carnage was considerable; several of the rebels who survived were later hanged in Glastonbury High Street.

The town's most notable and obvious landmark is the Tor, a conical natural hill which rises steeply a few hundred yards to the east. I say it is natural, but it is ringed by peculiar terraces that are obviously man-made. Legends abound here also. For some, the Tor is the hill of the fairies, and it contains the entrance to the underworld. You can drive most of the way to it, but I chose to walk up from the town; an excellent footpath starts at Dod Lane, off Chilkwell St, and progresses up through Bushy Coombe. It leads eventually to the road where cars are parked. Above this, the Tor itself, crowned by St Michael's Tower, looms spectacularly.

On this particular day, plenty of people were inspecting the tower, and the terraces immediately beneath it. But I had not met anybody on the footpath up from Dod Lane. On the way back down, however, I did meet a party of French schoolchildren, led by a very large Frenchman carrying a staff and sweating profusely. It would have been pleasant to have regarded him as some latter-day Joseph of Arimathea, but the conceit was not plausible. He bade me good day, asked how far there was to go, and then enjoined—I think—his flock not to give up. I thought that he was the one person in the party who looked like giving up, but he led nobly on.

And then I moved on to Cheddar, which was altogether more commercialised. Indeed, I had been warned that the southern—village—end of its celebrated gorge is scarred by some of the most crass exploitation of tourists in England; but although an amazing number of enterprises—including a "cheese depot", a "bazaar", fish and chip shops, a chicken bar, cafés and a cafeteria, tea shops, gift and craft shops, a "cave shop", licensed bars, a hotel, a tourist information centre and a museum—are all squeezed in beside the bottom end of the road that winds through the fissure, I did not find overmuch tattiness.

For £4 you could buy an inclusive ticket providing entry to the various caves and the "fantasy grotto", the museum and exhibition, and "Jacob's Ladder". Or you could pay separately if you did not wish to visit them all.

I climbed up the "ladder". At the top there is a small tower, and nearby is Pulpit Rock, offering slightly disappointing views into the gorge. But as you walk on, along the paths high above the gorge, views of the surrounding Somerset countryside open up, and they are splendid. Once again, I noted that people tended to cluster round the designated "attractions"; beyond Pulpit Rock, I had the place to myself.

From Cheddar I moved across to Wiltshire, and that night I stayed at Chilvester Hill House, just outside Calne. Unlike Chedington Court, which is unashamedly a hotel, if a very discreet one, Chilvester Hill House is definitely *not* a hotel.

Its owners, Dr and Mrs Dilley, are members of Wolsey Lodges, an organisation based in Suffolk. (The reference to Wolsey is because Cardinal Wolsey, Henry VIII's right-hand-man till that most gross of English kings turned on him, was a *bon viveur* who toured England expecting to receive generous hospitality wherever he pitched up. The parallel with today's Wolsey Lodges breaks down, however, when you recall that the cardinal did not expect to pay for his accommodation.)

The Wolsey Lodges brochure, entitled "Welcome To An Englishman's Home", explains that "meeting your host and hostess and their other guests is all part of the Wolsey Lodge experience . . . your hostess will usually have two or three bedrooms available for visitors . . . sometimes you share the family sitting-room, sometimes there is a special sitting-room for guests . . . staying at a Wolsey Lodge is a social experience . . . we would like to emphasise that a Wolsey Lodge is a home, not a hotel . . . as a guest in a private house, you have privileges and also obligations, just as you do when staying with relatives or friends . . . on arrival it is a good idea to ring the bell as you do at a home, rather than walk in as you would at a hotel . . . usually you will eat at a table with your hosts and their other guests . . . a few Wolsey Lodges have separate tables . . . Wolsey Lodge hostesses, and some hosts too, take pride in their cooking and in creating a friendly dinner party atmosphere"—and so on.

What is omitted in all this of course, is any reference to the fact that the guest is a *paying* guest; thus the experience, however "social", is not exactly akin to staying with relatives or friends.

I had misgivings about the entire Wolsey Lodge concept; it looked to me like a dangerous concoction of snobbery and pretence compounded by an almost childish conspiracy to obscure the commercial nature of the transaction between guest and host.

But these misgivings evaporated at Chilvester Hill House, such was the sheer force of the Dilleys' charm and kindness. They disarmed me, not by stealth as the Chapmans had at Chedington, but by a full assault on my sensibilities and prejudices. The Dilleys were larger than life, to the point of being overpowering; yet I defy anyone to dislike them.

Dr Dilley, a "semi-retired occupational physician" as he describes himself, came bounding out to greet me even as I parked my car (he was not satisfied with my parking and asked me to repark it) so I did not have to remind myself to have the "good idea" of ringing the bell. He explained that I was the first to arrive; the other guests that evening were a gent from the City, who was undergoing a "high-powered, one-to-one" computer course at nearby Swindon, and two American sisters, one from San Francisco, the other from Omaha, who were touring England.

I was allowed into the kitchen (a most unusual dispensation, I gathered) to chat with Gill Dilley as she prepared dinner. She confessed quite candidly that when her husband had "semi-retired" eight years previously, they had decided to move to the country but they did *not* want to move to some little bungalow. They could not afford a big country house; but she reckoned that if they bought a reasonably-sized one, and took visitors, then "the visitors would heat the house and feed the cattle". (Gill breeds cattle, though at present she has just four cows and a steer. They were ruminating contentedly in a field by the house when I arrived.)

The Dilleys fell in love with Chilvester Hill House, a Victorian mansion near the A4, as soon as they saw it. They bought it, and have never looked back. Indeed, the entries about Chilvester in various guides, including the *Good Hotel* (oops, that forbidden word) *Guide* and the *Which? Hotel* (that word again) *Guide* are almost ecstatic; I was, that evening, to learn why.

Gill Dilley told me that some people arrived and were perturbed to learn that there was no choice of menu. "Even though we are careful to inform people when they phone that there is no choice—and that we dine at eight. We can recommend plenty of places near here if people want to eat later."

I suggested to her that surely, over eight years, there had been occasions when their guests had not jelled; there must have been at least the occasional personality clash over dinner. She flatly denied it. But there had been some fairly droll, not to say rum, mixes. The most unlikely had been the night a Swiss chocolate salesman and his "dolly" sat down to dinner with a judge—but everything had "worked a treat". She conceded, however, that she and her husband sometimes had to work very hard to create the correct, ameliorative, atmosphere.

We had moved on to the notion of "service", and she was telling me that she currently had excellent helpers, but in the past there had been problems. "I've had some bad experiences—girls who'd trot up to the pink bedroom and sit there smoking, thinking I didn't know what was going on behind my back. But I did, I did."

At this point my fellow guest, the gent from the City, crashed in from the garden. Possibly he thought that a pre-dinner chat in the kitchen was a convention of the house. Mrs Dilley appeared momentarily discomfited, but rose to the occasion; soon we were discussing what wine should be chosen for dinner.

My new colleague, something of a wine buff, was talking about Lebanese wines and he mentioned a Lebanese vintner, Serge Hochar, who had done, he said, a great propaganda job for the wines of his country, despite all that wretched land's troubles.

At which Mrs Dilley said: "Yes, I used to go riding with him at the Sporting Club in Beirut." I could see that it was going to be that kind of evening: wide-ranging, exuberant and even baroque.

The American ladies desisted from entering the kitchen, but they proved excellent company over dinner. I quizzed them about their experiences of England, which proved to have been entirely favourable. They even praised the transport arrangements in London; they could not understand why such a fuss was made about the state of the Tube. They had found London pleasant and easy to move around in. They had a hired car, and were full of praise for English road manners. Eventually, under pressure from me, they did produce one minuscule complaint: the restaurants opened at odd times.

Our meal that evening was simple, yet rich, and cooked with classic English straightforwardness. Smoked fish; lamb with Jersey Royal potatoes, courgettes and broccoli; and rhubarb fool. And we enjoyed excellent wines chosen by my friend. The Dilleys left us to ourselves during the meal, but after dinner, over coffee and malt whisky in the sitting-room, they joined us. There was much excellent chat, not to say banter.

The next morning the City gent and Dr Dilley had both departed early (Dr Dilley still works, on a consultancy basis, for various companies). The American ladies were overjoyed with their visit; it had been the highlight of their vacation.

When I settled my bill, there was no reference to any wine. Mrs Dilley told me that my fellow guest had insisted on paying for all the wine because he had chosen it and had drunk most of it. The former was true; the latter was false. I departed quite disarmed; all my scepticism, my incipient animus, had vanished.

My final stop, before returning briefly to Scotland to see my wife and daughter, was Longleat. I wanted to visit a stately home, and what better than the very first one to be opened to the public? Longleat is also the site of the controversial safari park opened by the Marquess of Bath—with some assistance from Jimmy Chipperfield—amid much recrimination in 1966.

Nothing had prepared me for the overwhelming magnificence of the approach to Longleat through Heaven's Gate. I drove slowly through mature woodland, and then suddenly, through the "gate"—a gap in the trees—a celestial vista exploded before my eyes.

Four hundred feet below was the house itself, almost totally hidden; alongside, its lake, and then the safari park, looking like an image from some African dream, with exotic animals prowling the pasture. Everywhere, great trees and rolling parkland. Far beyond, the English landscape, green upon green, stretched to the horizon.

The road curves down, swinging through this divine landscape, laid out many many years ago by Lancelot "Capability" Brown, the supreme exponent of "artful wilderness". This is surely an approach to be made in an open, horse-drawn carriage, to music by Handel.

My approach was more mundane. Although the great acres of parkland are open to the public, I noticed at once that everyone was clustered round the house itself. Here were many attractions; a narrow-gauge railway, pleasure boats on the lake, a *Dr Who* exhibition, a butterfly garden, Postman Pat's corner, shops, a pub, and much more. As 1991 was the year of the maze, I plumped for that feature.

The Longleat maze was planted as recently as 1975. It is supposed to be the world's largest, and most difficult; it is flanked by 16,180 yew trees. You are supposed to reach the tower in the middle; less intrepid visitors may content themselves with merely finding the way out. I have to confess that after twenty minutes I happily opted for just that. Meanwhile a group of Germans had gained the tower and were loudly encouraging—or discouraging, more like it—the lesser mortals beneath them.

I then toured the Elizabethan house; splendid in its own way, but hardly comparable with the glorious landscape that surrounds it. I suspect that I share Dr Johnson's unease at displays of wealth by the aristocracy. I was also conscious—who could not be?—of the "upstairs, downstairs" syndrome. All these ostentatious pieces had been cleaned and looked after in the past by exploited drudges.

Christopher Hibbert, in his fine book *The English: A Social History 1066-1945*, recounts the duties of a housemaid at Longleat 160 years ago.

> The dustpans were all numbered: each housemaid had her own and had to learn how to hold it, together with a candle, in one hand so that she could use the brush with the other. She also had to learn how to polish the metal fittings on furniture with fine sand, how to polish paintwork with cream dressing, how to sweep carpets with damp tea leaves, how to take off old polish with vinegar and put on new with beeswax and turpentine; how to wash high ceilings with soda and water while standing on the top of stepladders; how to dust down brocaded walls and rub them over with tissue paper and and then with silk dusters; how to unstring and scrub Venetian blinds; how to take up carpets; how to whiten corridors with pipeclay and spread French chalk on the floor before a ball: how to make a bed and black a bedroom grate with a mixture of ivory black, treacle, oil, small beer and sulphuric acid. She also had to remember at what time the sunlight came into various rooms so that the blinds could be drawn to protect the furniture. And she was very poorly paid.

To be fair to the present Lord Bath, however, the finery and riches on display were tempered with some quirky items; a display of cartoons about Longleat, for example, and a portrait of the Pools Panel, which he chaired for many years.

I then walked round the grounds; as I say, everyone was clustered in the vicinity of the house and its attendant facilities; as I wandered over the vast sweeps of parkland, I encountered only a single horseman and two girls walking an Alsatian.

I departed Longleat on a golden, mellow evening, still wondering at its splendour, and drove on to Bristol, where I was to put my car on the MotorRail service to Scotland. The train did not arrive at Temple Meads Station till 11.15, so I had a little time to kill. The atmosphere in the station was less seedy than I had expected. The all-night bar was, for some reason, at the far side, on the furthest platform, reached by a long subway. This proved to be a well-lit, broad, white-tiled passageway that was impeccably clean.

In the bar were a few morose-looking night travellers; there was also one of those helpers which some bars attract—an old boy fussing around, collecting empties and generally trying to make himself useful. He attempted to help the steward with his crossword, then gave up. I supped a pint, observing this funereal scene, and then made my way back to the rather cramped lounge provided for the MotorRail passengers, where I was received by a pleasant girl and given a nice cup of tea, gratis. Temple Meads Station by night may lack glitz, but there must be many worse places in England.

CHAPTER NINE

VERSIONS OF ENGLAND

The Vicar

In recent years, England has been wracked by some much publicised child abuse scandals. One of these became known as the Rochdale case, although the children in question came from Langley, a housing estate on the other side of the M62 from Rochdale. Twenty children were taken into care in June 1990; in March 1991, sixteen of them were returned to their parents. At that time I heard the Rector of Langley, the Reverend Ian Johnson, speaking most movingly on the radio about the despair in the lives of the majority of his parishioners. Two months later, I decided to seek him out.

The Langley estate looks, superficially, green and pleasant. The motorway is to the north, and there is open country on two other sides. The houses are in neat terraces, and are only two storeys high. Hedges and grass are everywhere. It looks, yet again, like that typical English device, the town masquerading as the country. As you look more closely, Langley is squalid, even degrading.

Ian Johnson, a tall, bearded, intense man of forty-six, lives with his wife and three daughters in the rectory next to the modernistic All Saints Church. He was the most complex man I met on my journey round England; his experiences over the last decade encapsulate the acute division that splits England. Not, as he stresses, that between the north and the south, though he moved to Langley from the fatlands of Dorset, but rather that of Disraeli's two nations, the rich and the poor. This may seem hackneyed and obvious, but Ian Johnson knows well that it is one of the blights of modern England that those who are prospering, in many cases as never before, have no conception whatsoever of the lifestyles of deprived people living only a mile or so away from them. The deprivation may be to some extent self-imposed: no matter.

Ian Johnson himself experienced such a shock when he first ministered in Langley. He is still, three years on, grappling with the after-effects. He doesn't think that the division which separates Englishman from Englishman is merely about wealth and poverty, though that is at the core of it. "Monetary poverty, I suppose, can eventually be dealt with. Eventually, if there is the political will. But the people in Middleton, just down the road from here, they simply don't understand the poverty of opportunity in Langley, the sheer poverty of experience."

We chatted over tea in his study; then he took me for a tour of his parish; then we had a deep and protracted conversation in which he talked of the doubts that always overcame him when he spoke frankly about the community he serves. "My problem will always be that I am perceived as an outsider criticising the people here. But I don't feel superior. I feel vulnerable. I care for and love the people here."

We started our tour at the shopping mall almost opposite the rectory. Most of the shops were shuttered. A couple of taxis were waiting; children played happily enough amid the litter. Ian told me that one end of the mall was used for drug-dealing, the other end for prostitution. When they were in the mood the police would check anyone and everyone for drugs; an eighty-seven-year-old woman had been searched.

Then we drove around the estate. There was litter everywhere, some of it wedged deep into the hedges, which were unkempt and in some cases grotesquely overgrown. Many of the houses were boarded up. One had been scarred by a recent fire; half of its roof was gone. In the streets bricks and bottles and cans were scattered about. There were derelict cars and abandoned prams. The smaller but more mobile detritus of carryout meals was everywhere, blowing in the wind. We passed a children's play area which had been fenced off. A big red sign said: DANGER. Ian said that last year it was cleaned up at a cost of several thousand pounds; soon the broken glass, the condoms and the syringes were scattered across it again, and no child could possibly play there.

Here was a Church of England priest, in the early summer of 1991, taking me round his parish; not in a spirit of pride, but in a spirit of abject shame.

Ian Johnson comes from a comfortable middle-class background. He has been a priest for twenty years; seventeen of them in the rich, lush pastures of Dorset and Wiltshire, and the last three in the wastelands of Langley. He was a parish priest for five years in one of the wealthiest parishes in England; he also worked as a youth and education officer.

In that capacity he once organised a youth event in Salisbury Cathedral. "We had 1,500 youngsters in the cathedral for eighteen hours. There was beautiful lighting. The whole length of the nave, over 200 feet, was carpeted—just for that one event. We had marquees outside. The WRVS did the food. The cost of the project was enormous. The shortfall, all that we didn't raise ourselves, was made good by the Bishop of Salisbury. It was a big ego trip for me."

Knowing what he knows now about the other England, such an event must seem utterly frivolous to Ian Johnson.

He decided to move to a city parish when he was impressed by the Church of England's report, *Faith in the City*, on urban priorities. He was offered the leadership of the Langley team ministry. He looked round the place for twenty-four hours. Then he returned with his wife and they had another quick look. "And my wife said, as we were driving back down the motorway—'I don't see why we shouldn't.' But if we had looked a little longer and a little harder we certainly would not have come. If we had looked at the extent of the filth, at the dead dogs and the discarded syringes, we would not have come. No, if I had known the poverty of spirit here, the de-Christian nature of the church, the desperation of the place—if I had had my present knowledge, I would not have come."

But he did come. Evidently a priest in Manchester, who knew him vaguely, opened a book on how long Ian Johnson would last. "He has lost quite a lot of money by now!" he laughs.

Ian Johnson expected a welcome; he did not get it. "I was very aware that I had made sacrifices, and so had my family, to come. The people here didn't appreciate that at all."

His first months were terrible. He was often in despair. His curate left. He appointed a vicar to work with him. He lasted five months. "He just couldn't cope. He had eight months off after he left." Eventually, two good men joined Ian Johnson and the team ministry is now working well.

In the dark early months, he was convinced that his whole ministry would fail. He says that it was when he learned to come to terms with failure that he began to succeed. He clearly lowered his aspirations. At first he wanted to be tested, and thought he could change a lot quickly. Now he realises that in listening to someone over a cup of tea, he is maybe doing as much as he can in the particular circumstances.

He has also become harder. Each week about ten or fifteen people will appear at the rectory door, begging. At first he got angry, with himself as much as the beggars, when he turned them away. Now he does so in a more relaxed and friendly manner.

He is no longer moved by famine and catastrophe elsewhere in the world. "Ethiopia doesn't touch me any more. The problems are so pressing here." But he adds: "I have more hope now. I can survive this place and I can operate as a parish priest here. I can't do too much. But I do what I can. I no longer feel personally responsible for the state of the parish. If I did, I would need psychiatric treatment."

Nonetheless, the shock of his early months in Langley is still with him, inside him, a living thing. "I went to New Guinea when I was twenty-one. I can in all sincerity say that it was less of a culture shock than coming to Langley at forty-three. I really mean that. And it's just four hours up the motorway."

He regularly returns to Dorset and Wiltshire. "I know that the people with whom I used to work there have not the slightest idea of what this place is like. Of course they do see places like this on the telly from time to time, but it's just not real to them."

After three years of growing success, in personal terms, he still doesn't understand the people of Langley.

"There are some scoundrels. But most of them are nice, warm, people.

But . . .

I can't understand what makes a mother feed her children on nothing but chips and crisps when it makes them constipated and it would be cheaper to cook a twenty-minute meal . . .

I can't understand what makes a woman of forty keep several alsatians in a first floor flat, and never take them out . . .

I can't understand what allows a mother to let her child of five watch telly until he falls asleep in front of it each and every night . . .

I can't understand what makes a family rip all the copper piping out of their home to sell it at a ridiculously low price."

He then told me about a funeral he had taken that week. A young woman of twenty-six, a mother of two, had thrown herself in front of a lorry. Her father told Ian Johnson her despair had been so great, it was the best thing that could have happened.

Ian has had to deal with about twelve suicides in Langley. In the south, he handled six in seventeen years. He is still shocked by the number of funerals he has to take. "Men in their fifties, men who would have expected to live another twenty or thirty years in the south." They die of asbestosis and of heart disease.

He told me that nine out of ten baptisms in his church were of children of unmarried parents. Sometimes the father was not in evidence at all; it wasn't known who he was.

I said that, without being mawkish, I had been ashamed of my gender when I was talking to Doreen, the abandoned mother, in London.

He said that in Langley, he was amazed at what women suffered. He knew of one woman who had several cleaning jobs, in a pub, a school and a factory, yet she still managed to get her kids to school and cook them meals. The husband drank all day in various pubs (Langley is well served by pubs).

"I am appalled at the abuse, mental and physical, that the women receive. Some of the men treat their women as chattels, no more. I have seen a drunk man dragging a woman home by her hair."

But he despairs most of the children. He told me of very young children who could tell you what was on telly at four in the morning. He told me of a dental inspection in one of the Langley primary schools. Several young children in each class had severe septicaemia. But their parents refused free dental treatment. They were not going to allow the authorities, whether they were dentists, social workers or police, to interfere.

I reminded him that I had first heard him speaking in the aftermath of the child abuse furore. He said that he was still ministering to the parents, and did not wish to say anything on the record. But from what he had said earlier, I think he feels that many of the children in Langley would live a happier and more normal life if they were "in care". Many of the children in Langley were certainly deprived of a family life, in the traditional sense of the phrase. They had TV meals instead of family meals, and so on.

Ian Johnson measures the desperation and degradation of his parish in many ways; one of the worst, he says, is that there is no desire for education. There were 1,300 primary children in Langley, but only seven sixth form pupils. "They just don't want to be educated, as you or I would understand the term."

I asked about racial tensions on the estate; he said there were none, for the simple reason that almost everyone was white. "The blacks don't want to come here," he said. "Far more resources go to places that are multi-racial." When I asked about unemployment, he urged me to be cautious, for there was a large "black economy", mainly consisting of women making shirts or cleaning. The latest statistics indicated that 70 per cent of the young people, those aged from sixteen to twenty-four, were unemployed.

I invited him to analyse the cause of all this, but he told me that he had long since put such attempts aside. All he knew was, and he used the word advisedly, that it was "evil" for human beings to feel that they did not matter. English society had failed most of the people of Langley completely.

Ian Johnson is, as I said, a complex man. He is probably as near to being a saint as anyone I met on my journey. By that I don't mean that he *is* a saint. He has however given up, or discarded, a lot of personal luggage in Langley, certainty, optimism, comfort. He is a wiser and more realistic and more fulfilled man than he was three years ago.

It would be wrong to present him as an embattled, middle-class emigré, the scourge of wanton and feckless Northerners. He is not like that at all. He is rather a typical privileged Englishman, utterly ill-prepared by his upbringing, his education and his previous prosperous environment to confront what parts of his own country have become.

Sometimes he seemed to me to be veering towards self-pity, but he would veer away again before he reached that negative state. He has certainly suffered in his time at Langley, and he still bears the psychological scars of his early, wretched, months. He does not pretend to know the place well, or to understand its people. But he has learned to care for them. Only once in our conversation did he become bitter. That was when he said: "The Church of England has ratted on Langley. They should have at least seven or eight people here."

Late in 1990, John Major stood at the front door of Number 10 Downing Street as the new Prime Minister. He spoke of his vision of a classless society, of a country at ease with itself. Ian Johnson's forty-six years amount to a life in a country that is desperately divided. His story is of an England that is manifestly not classless, that is manifestly not at ease with itself.

The Brewer

A few miles away from bracing Skegness is Wainfleet, an old redbrick town, once the Roman town of Vainona and a great port, but now noted for its small but distinguished brewery.

You find the brewery at Salem Bridge, beside a windmill. This is where the Bateman beers—"Good Honest Ales" is their slogan—on sale throughout Lincolnshire and, increasingly, elsewhere, have been produced for more than a hundred years. Batemans is a clean, happy, well-ordered workplace. But there is a sad family story here.

The current chairman, George Bateman, was told in 1985—eleven years after the brewery had celebrated its centenary—that his brother and sister, who owned 60 per cent of the company, no longer wished to continue with the business. There followed an intensive struggle which divided the family and which eventually saw the forces of good—brewing is an emotive business—prevail and the brewery remain an independent family firm.

Or, as George Bateman himself puts it, with a tone of controlled and justifiable triumphalism: "Today the brewery is still in family hands and totally independent after George Bateman's two-year battle to ward off takeover bids from predators, which earned him the gratitude of his employees and the local community, as well as the esteem of his tenants and the approval of drinkers throughout England."

Now George Bateman, his wife Pat, their son Stuart and their daughter Jackie run the business—with a little help from such as Martin Cullimore, the head brewer, and Stuart Bell, the long-serving company secretary.

There are about forty brewing staff, another twenty work in the office and there are ten reps on the road.

Batemans produce about 550 barrels a week (a barrel is a term of volume signifying 288 pints. Most of the Batemans beer is sold in either kilderkins or firkins, casks of 144 and 72 pints respectively).

The ambience of an old-fashioned family firm—or even a superior Victorian counting-house—is established as you walk into the reception area, where a clerk is sitting at a high stool, working at a huge well-varnished desk.

Martin Cullimore, who is to show me round, appears. An enthusiastic Welshman of thirty-seven, he wears a clean white coat and carries a portable phone. Brewing Bateman-style is a judicious blend of the traditional and the technological.

As a somewhat dazed veteran of several distillery tours, I have not yet learned to understand the complex processes which culminate in such ambrosian final products. But brewing does seem simpler than distilling. The basic ingredients are of course barley, hops and yeast. The barley is reduced to malt (Batemans use Pipkin malt, supplied by six different maltsters). Twenty farms in Kent and Worcestershire provide the hops.

Despite his immense knowledge of brewing, Martin is unable to explain to me exactly what a hop is: he settles for "a sort of cross between a fruit and a herb". Anyway, hops are grown on poles, like vines, and their little yellow-green cones give English beer its marvellous bitterness. Martin lets me crush some of these tiny cones in my hand; the aroma is tangy and strange.

The third ingredient, yeast, is a fungus, but it is essential to the brewing process. Each brewery has its own unique strain of yeast; the culture is carefully guarded in the brewery laboratory.

As we tour the brewery, we climb up and down various ladders and peer into various vats, filled with mash and fermenting beer. I am greatly impressed by the cleanliness of the plant.

Martin explains to me another ingredient: isinglass, a special type of protein extracted from fish, which is used to combine with the yeast to make cask beer settle better.

Martin Cullimore is a science graduate, as are the three brewers who work under him. As a scientific illiterate, I am relieved when we end up in the sample room, a somewhat austere enclave at the rear of the brewery. Here I am to be rewarded for my concentration. For Batemans brew superb beer. It is not just me, an appreciative ignoramus, who says so. It is not just Batemans blowing their own trumpet. The Campaign for Real Ale, that most commendable of English pressure-groups, has granted Batemans many awards and commendations. Indeed, at the height of the brewery's battle to retain its independence, its Triple X bitter won the Champion Beer of Britain award.

What we are about to enjoy is not the proverbial piss-up in a brewery (which so many politicians apparently could not organise) but a judicious tasting.

Martin pours me some XB bitter—which I had already sampled in various parts of Lincolnshire—and some XXXB bitter. Let me quote Roger Protz, a better judge than I will ever be, on the qualities of those beers:

XB Bitter—Nose: Delicate grain and hop aromas, slight orange fruit notes. Palate: Light, refreshing balance of grain and hop with long dry finish. Summary: A rounded ale of distinction. *XXXB Bitter*—Nose: Lovely wafts of hop resin and jammy fruit. Palate: Fat malt in the mouth with deep rounded finish and sultana and vanilla notes. Summary: Superb, complex premium bitter, fine companion for ripe cheese.

As we sample this nectar, Martin tells me of his own background. "Brewing picked me rather than the other way round. I had a biochemistry degree from Liverpool University and no job. I applied for all sorts of things, including a job at Mansfield Brewery. I got that one, and became a brewer."

He had to serve a five-year apprenticeship and then sit the Institute of Brewing exams—"much more arduous than my degree"—before he could call himself a brewer.

We discuss English attitudes to beer, that most supremely English of drinks. "The English have not taken enough interest in their beer," says Martin, categorically. "They are not patriotic enough." I ask him to explain.

He believes that beer is much less glamorous than wine because people who enjoy beer—and people have been enjoying this wholesome English drink since before the Romans came—don't make a fuss about it. "They just get on and drink it."

But in these days of hype, of consumer pundits and taste gurus, beer is willy-nilly going to require a higher profile. Beer writers such as Michael Jackson and Roger Protz are becoming as well known as wine writers. CAMRA has emerged. Good luck to them all.

We turn to the contentious topic of lager. Martin suggests that the English public have been duped into thinking that the weak, bland, gassy beer they are offered as lager is like good continental lager, which he characterises as delightful and strong. He wouldn't walk round the corner for a British lager, he says.

I then invoke the lager lout syndrome. If English lager is so weak, how does he explain the rise of the lout? "It's unfair to blame that on lager," he says. "They may start off with a few pints of lager but then they move on to shorts."

Martin has a seven-year-old daughter—so have I—and he produces what strikes me as a most apt analogy as we discuss lager drinking. "It's like teaching my daughter to read. Many lager drinkers are in the 17–22 age range. Their tastes will mature. Our English lager is the beer equivalent of nursery rhymes."

And your best bitter is the equivalent of Shakespeare? "Exactly."

We talk about the lost county of Lincoln—Martin's view is that it is not even dismissed by most English people because it never occurs to them in the first place—and then return to the resentment which is smouldering somewhere deep in this otherwise affable man. "The English do not make nearly enough of the fact that their great traditional drink is ale. We still have sixty breweries producing good ale. It's a shame that the public thinks so little of a homegrown product they should be really proud of."

As a parting gift he hands me three bottles of XXXB. Clutching them, I walk past the windmill, through gentle hoppy wafts, and set off again on my travels.

The Publican

Doncaster is a gritty, no-nonsense working town, but drive out of it past the magnificent race-course—home of the St Leger—and you are suddenly in its posh ossified hinterland. Here are the archetypal leafy avenues of suburbia: detached houses with big gardens and extraordinary notices saying Burglars Beware. (Should it not be the other way round? Or are burglars being warned that here retribution is swift and salutary? That the local residents are prepared to take the law into their own hands?)

As you turn east towards the M18 motorway you reach open land: big fields and big farms. Yet this is very much leisure country; the narrow lanes are busy with joggers, cyclists and horsewomen. Larks are singing and in the distance a dog barks persistently. The throb of the M18 traffic is barely audible. The sky is big and blue. In Branton, a ragged village, a man is intently hosing, not his car or his lawn, but his tarmac drive. Is this mere English eccentricity, or an example of the national profligacy with water?

The Three Horse Shoes public house, a neat white-washed building by the main road, stands gleaming in the sun. It looks solid and welcoming; but all is not well within.

At first, no problems are apparent. It is a big pub, with plenty of seats around the island bar. In one corner is a telly, festooned with sporting cups and trophies. Under it are three Union Jacks with the bombastic pun—"These Colours Don't Run".

Three ladies are busy hoovering, wiping, dusting, getting ready for opening time. By the bar, sipping his coffee, stands a dark, dapper, middle-aged man, sporting a moustache and wearing his hair quite long at the back. He is Terry Hamilton, forty-six, landlord of the Three Horse Shoes for the past nine years.

During this time he has established himself as the orchestrator of community life and Branton's biggest employer. He employs seven part-time bar staff, in addition to his wife Denise and his daughter Amanda and his son Alaster.

Terry says that every minute he's awake he's working and, as he talks you through his working week, you begin to believe it. A small example: he cashes about twenty cheques a week, and not just during opening hours. People knock at the door at nine in the morning, wanting cash for their shopping in Doncaster.

The pub is very much a focus of sporting activity. Terry is a former professional footballer, with Lincoln City, and he is chairman of the pub's football club and its golf society. Denise, a keen horsewoman, organises sponsored charity rides each bank holiday. All the time, they are raising money for various charities: "It doesn't just come, you have to push," says Terry.

When the working man's club down the road—one of Terry's local rivals—was burgled, Terry immediately offered an interest-free loan of £3,000. It was not taken up because the insurance money came through quickly, but Terry is proud of his local role. He is not so much a philanthropist as a certainty, the figure everybody relies on.

His standards are high. Although the pub gets very busy, especially at weekends, he insists on no swearing. "When I came here, everybody swore." He claims he always knows what's going on in every part of the bar and you believe him. He refuses to pander to the cruder tastes of the local youths: he will not sell snake bites (a nightmare mixture of bitter and cider) nor will he allow drinking direct from the bottle, a custom that is evidently tolerated in some Doncaster pubs.

Terry has no problems with lager louts, partly because he doesn't sell all that much lager. "Youngsters like lager because it's cold and consistent. But I serve a consistent standard of bitter." Terry explains the lager lout phenomenon thus: "If I had flashing lights, then I would get trouble. When you have 500 young people together and empty them onto the street at the same time you are asking for trouble."

He has a lot of young customers, but he also has a lot of young middle-aged. "The youngsters I inherited," as he puts it. They are now married and heavily mortgaged. And like all good publicans, he has a fair proportion of older customers. Many of them travel to the pub from surrounding villages and from Doncaster.

Terry is a tenant of Bass. Before he and Denise took over the Three Horse Shoes nine years ago, he had been a district manager with the brewer for twelve years.

Then one day he was "gutted", as he puts it, to receive from Bass a photocopied letter saying that the Three Horse Shoes was to become a managed house. The brewer said he could apply for tenancy at another house. He was offered compensation of £22,000 to leave—much less than he had personally spent on refurbishments.

As Terry tells me this, he allows himself, for the only moment in our conversation, to become bitter. "A tenancy at another house," he says. "Oh yes. And I build up the trade again. And in a few years I am told, once again—you're out."

A tenancy at another house seems scant reward for a man who has more than doubled the pub's custom in nine years; who has spent many thousands of pounds of his own money on new fittings and furnishings, who has built a patio and created a beer garden, who has become the *animateur* in the community, who has, in short, created a prime local amenity.

But therein lies the strength of Terry's position: "I have had tremendous support. Everybody is talking about a petition. But I want to hold off. I want to negotiate. I want the brewer to see reason." He is well aware of the power of publicity, and he insists that if it does come to the stage when the brewer calls in the bailiffs, then he will have a thousand people outside the pub, and he and his family will go, kicking and screaming, before the TV cameras.

Terry Hamilton was born in Lancashire and brought up in Lincolnshire. He is a courteous man, and a reasonable one. "I can see the brewer's problem," he says. "But it isn't fair, the way they are going about this." Terry Hamilton's case is not untypical. All across England long-serving landlords are being threatened with eviction. This is because of a Monopolies and Mergers Commission report which ordered brewers to sell large parts of their tied estates. The brewers are therefore trying to turn profitable tenancies into managed houses. It is the bigger and better run and more profitable pubs which are being seized for direct management. Bass alone is transferring 580 pubs from tenancy to direct management. In many cases, the tenants who have built up these businesses feel that the compensation they are being offered is derisory.

Thus that most rewarding and typical of all English institutions, the pub, becomes the depository of disillusion, even despair.

The Parliamentarian

Redfield Lane is a discreet, almost furtive, little street in West London, not far from Earl's Court. Taxi drivers who have "done the knowledge" still have to consult their *A–Z*s to find it. It is almost spookily quiet, considering that one of London's busiest road junctions—where Earl's Court Road intersects Cromwell Road—is only a hundred yards away. Here, tucked away beside a delightful secret garden, is the home of one of England's most distinguished Parliamentarians, the Rt Hon. Dr John Gilbert.

Everything about Dr Gilbert suggests a mandarin Tory of the old school. A tall man, he speaks with a slight drawl. He has the old-fashioned good looks of a matinee idol of the 1950s, and a gently patrician air. His table talk is at once elegant, amusing, pungent—occasionally waspish. He was once named by the *Sunday Express* as one of Britain's richest men; he denies that he is even a millionaire, but admits to being "comfortably off"— he does a lot of consultancy work. He is fascinated by, and at ease in, the world of international finance. But of all the political issues that have exercised him, defence is the one that has, and continues to, concern him most. He was a consistent, outspoken and eloquent scourge of the Labour Party's unilateralism of the early 1980s.

But Dr Gilbert is not a Conservative. He is a Labour MP, albeit an exceedingly independent-minded one. On the night he and his wife Jean entertained me to a splendid dinner, he recounted that the previous weekend he had received a cake from his grateful constituency party in Dudley East, marking his twenty-one years' service as an MP.

John Gilbert is one of the last of the old-style Parliamentarians, a man not easily pigeon-holed or categorised. He is best known to the public at large as a master interrogator who has used the select committees, reintroduced to Parliament by Norman St John Stevas in 1979, with consummate, forensic skill.

His most celebrated moments came in 1986, when he was the star of the Defence Select Committee's exhaustive investigation into the Westland debacle. Mrs Thatcher's Government came close to collapsing over Westland; it was Dr Gilbert, more than anyone else, who brought it to the brink.

He retains his touch; he is now on the Trade and Industry Committee, and on the evening of our dinner he was still smarting because a few days earlier he had been prevented by the acting chairman, Robin Maxwell-Hyslop, from going in for the kill when he had a Cabinet Minister, Peter Lilley, on the rack. Mind you, he had already reduced the minister to gibbering incoherence by the simple expedient of requesting him, with seeming innocence, but dogged persistence, to define the term asset-stripper. Whoever coined the phrase "iron hand in the velvet glove" could well have had Dr Gilbert in mind.

In the 1970s John Gilbert himself served as a minister: he was Financial Secretary to the Treasury, and Minister for Transport. He now describes himself as being utterly bereft of ambition and completely independent in spirit. They are not bad credentials for a backbench MP.

John Gilbert was rusticated from Oxford "for doing no work". During his time there he attended just three lectures. "I went on and got a PhD in international economics elsewhere, just to show them that I had a brain." He explains his disillusion with lectures at Oxford thus: "You would sit beside an unwashed woman on an old wooden bench listening, or attempting to listen, to some ancient bore giving an inaudible address." He contrasts this with his later experience as a lecturer at various American universities. "There you were challenged constantly. Some youngster would interrupt you when you'd hardly started. Then he'd sit back, a pencil in his mouth, and hear out your reply to his point. Then he'd say: 'OK, I'll buy that.' And you felt great."

As well as his economics doctorate, John Gilbert has several banking and accountancy qualifications. "An economist who can't read a balance sheet is no use whatsoever. Unfortunately, we have rather a lot of them in England."

He lived and worked in North America for twelve years and describes himself as "classic mid-Atlantic man". He quotes Benjamin Franklin: "Every man has two countries. His own and France," and adds: "That may well be true of most Englishmen. But for me, the second country has to be the US."

He believes that the English have tended to take for granted the American contribution to their defence over the past two generations. Further, he thinks that on the Continent that contribution is not just taken for granted: it is actively resented. When we had dinner, the Yugoslav crisis had just blown up and the Luxembourg Foreign Minister, one M. Poos, had told the Americans not to get involved, saying it was a European problem and one for Europeans to resolve. Dr Gilbert waxed indignant. "The impudence of the man! He and his like have been defended by the Americans for over forty years, and this is his response! What shall I call this man Poos? A puffed-up poof?"

Not that Dr Gilbert is an unthinking admirer of the US. He likens the current American attitude to Japan to that of the English to the Americans in the 1950s and 1960s: "Resentment, in a word. The Japanese are doing everything so much better, teaching the Americans lessons."

He reckons that anti-Americanism was the curse of British public life in the 1950s and 1960s. "People like Ted Heath and Roy Jenkins were profoundly anti-American. There was an irritation at the end of the Empire, a longing for a new role, and a resentment that focused on the Americans.

"I was born in 1927 and I can well remember when I was twelve, how much of the world map was still coloured red. The English middle classes were brought up to think that everything in England was of the highest quality, and that the Empire would continue to nurture this way of life for them. We treated the Empire rather like the Soviets treated the Comecon countries.

"And what lost us the Empire? In a way, people who could not handle servants. The real rub, all over the world, came when white met black. The major source of friction, again all over the world, was when English people could not handle their servants. They didn't know how to.

"I particularly blame the wives. It went on till quite recently, maybe is still going on in some places. I certainly saw it in the hills of Jamaica not all that long ago. I have seen white people shouting at their servants in such a way that you want to get up and hit them. Then, when they arrived back here, these same people could not afford servants. Maybe that was just as well, but it all amounted to a potent brew of resentment and bitterness. And now, a generation on, far too many Englishmen will tell you why you can't do this or you can't do that. The smallness of England these days appals me. People seem to relish telling you why such and such a thing cannot be, or should not be, attempted."

I asked him what symbolised England for him. He thought

hard and said that the good characteristics of the English were probably self-deprecation, and an enormous sense of privacy. But as for a symbol, he needed to think for some time.

Eventually he came up with: Rolls-Royce. And he talked of the great shock to English self-esteem when Rolls-Royce had to be rescued from bankruptcy by the Heath Government in 1971, by being taken into the public sector: not so much a nationalisation as a sort of privatisation in reverse.

At this point Jean Gilbert interrupted our conversation to say that surely the great symbol of England was its countryside; the beautiful pastoral landscape, with its lovely villages. This did not cut much ice with her husband, who is more of a townie.

He enjoys powerful motor cars, and he has controversial views on transport policy. (He recalls that the most amazing thing that ever happened to him in politics occurred when he was Transport Minister in 1975. A fellow Labour Minister—he refuses to name him—told him that there was absolutely nothing wrong with Britain's existing road infrastructure, and that it did not require any significant investment programme for the future.)

This articulate man is rendered almost speechless by such attitudes. His belief in the motor car is passionate: "The car is used, and needed, by ordinary people. It is most certainly not an elitist form of transport. Who opposed the motorways built in England? Not ordinary people, not working people, but middle class louts. UMCLOUTS, I call them. Upper middle class louts. You saw them breaking up motorway inquiries—bearded, besandaled, but louts nonetheless. For some reason the idea of a four-lane motorway remains immoral and disgusting to many middle class Englishmen. My goodness, it's like staying up after ten o'clock! You see, the motorways were driven through middle class, often upper middle class, areas. I predicted a long time ago that if you wanted to build a railway through such areas, you'd get the same twisted reaction. It was not really a car versus train issue at all. And, sure enough, look what happened in Kent when they wanted to build the new rail link for the Channel Tunnel. The Umclouts came crawling out of the woodwork all over again."

Although he maintains a house in Dudley, and excellent relations with his constituents—he has easily seen off putative attempts from the extreme Left to deselect him—he delights in London with an enthusiasm he cannot muster for the West Midlands.

He claims, enjoying the paradox, that he loves London because he is an internationalist. "It remains an extraordinarily international city. If you want an expert—a real expert, not a charlatan—on anywhere, absolutely anywhere, in the world, you will find one in London. Not even New York or Washington can provide the same assembled international knowledge that you can find here."

John Gilbert is a man whom the Labour Party—of which he remains very fond, despite the last ten years—could have made more use of. His contribution to public life is by no means extinguished, and he'd make a superb British ambassador to Washington—if anyone had the imagination to appoint him.

He always lacked the pugnacious, bruising style—and the ambition—of one of his closest colleagues in politics, Denis Healey (of whom he speaks with enormous affection and a little mischief, even confessing to dining out on Denis Healey jokes). He says simply: "Denis Healey was head and shoulders above both Wilson and Callaghan."

John Gilbert never played for the high political stakes that Healey played for; he was obviously never a potential leader of his party. But he always spoke his mind, over defence in particular, to the extent than on occasion he managed to infuriate Margaret Thatcher and Neil Kinnock at the same time.

"Defence," he insists, "must always be one of the cornerstones of our public life. But very few people in the Commons—and I'm not just talking about the Labour Party—take a serious interest in defence. You'd be surprised how few Tories do.

"For Labour MPs, for far too long, it has not been respectable

DORSET

KATE GERAGHTY

Skegness

Henry Thorold, Squire of Marston

Lincoln Cathedral

Woodhall Spa

Brighton Beach

CANAL SCENE, STOKE

IAN JOHNSON (RIGHT) AND PARISHIONERS

Tan Hill Inn, Yorkshire

Crewe Station

DOVER CASTLE

Farmer Stuart Yarwood, Cheshire

Leslie Illingworth

to take the defence of their country seriously. But that is at last changing. As my colleague Bruce George said to me the other day: 'John, they are giving us our party back.'"

The Club

The Garrick, now one of London's most fashionable clubs, has had an eventful history, punctuated by scandal and dispute. Founded in 1831 by a dilettante called Francis Mills, it was named after the great actor David Garrick who had died half a century earlier. As Guy Boas notes in his history of the club, it possesses much that was Garrick's "from his birth certificate to his dress sword, from his wig powder puff to his fishing rod".

Although the Garrick rapidly became an institution, it always had a raffish rather than a staid persona. The founding idea had been "to establish a society in which actors and men of education and refinement might meet on equal terms". The snobbish implication there is that actors were not men of education and refinement; nonetheless, it was the conduct of early members who were *not* actors which seems to have left most to be desired.

Lord Roos was expelled for cheating at whist: John Foster, the biographer of Dickens, was attacked by a fellow member, the Rev. R. E. Barham, as "a low scribbler without an atom of talent". Another member had to resign after being accused by a housemaid of stealing soap.

The larger than life Alfred Bunn, a gross and bejewelled impresario who managed the Drury Lane and Covent Garden theatres in the 1840s, detested the Garrick. He wrote: "The club, shorn of its proper supporters, has degenerated into a sort of junior law club. At its tables congregate some of the *soi-disant* critics who gather together what little dramatic intelligence they deal in from the gabble and hoaxing of waggish bystanders, whose notions of actors' performances are usually derived from what they have heard a self-satisfied actor say of himself . . . the club affords many a malcontent the advantage of coals and candles gratis . . ."

This stream of jaundice might well have been connected with the facts that Bunn had failed to be elected to the club despite the support of the Duke of Beaufort; and that he had been physically assaulted by a celebrated member, the actor Macready. Not that Macready, despite his membership and his regular use of the Garrick, had a much more favourable view of it.

"Dined at the Garrick, really a blackguard place," he confided to his diary. And again: "Dined at the Garrick, where the principal conversation is eating, drinking or the American presidency. It really is a disgusting place." Again: "Was going to dine at the Garrick, but reflecting I might get into heat with some of the low and vulgar frequenters of the place I ordered my chop in my room." Again: "Ate a sandwich at the Garrick, which gave me a headache."

But all this seems small beer beside the notorious feud that developed between the Garrick's two most celebrated members, Dickens and Thackeray, over a third member, Edmund Yates, a journalist.

Yates had written, in a weekly called *Town Tavern*, some offensive paragraphs about Thackeray, based on his observations of the novelist's behaviour at the Garrick. Yates refused to apologise; Thackeray reported him to the club committee; Yates was expelled. (He later went to prison for libelling a member of another club.)

Dickens, who was godfather to one of Yates's children, was disgusted by what he regarded as Thackeray's hypersensitivity and high-handed over-reaction, and refused to speak to his fellow-novelist for fifteen years.

After Dickens and Thackeray, the most famous Victorian member of this quintessentially English institution was another great novelist, Trollope, who was elected in 1862. As his view of England became darker and darker—just like that of Dickens before him—Trollope was undoubtedly influenced by what he heard in the smoking room of the club. But he loved the place: it was "the first assemblage of men at which I felt myself to be popular".

Trollope became, in his later years, increasingly deaf. One evening he and another deaf member were bawling at each other so loudly that other members, in all seriousness, threatened to call the police.

Proudly displayed in the Garrick is a letter Trollope wrote to Browning asking the poet to dine with him at the club. A footnote reveals, apparently without conscious irony, that Trollope was taken ill the day after the dinner, and died some weeks later.

Eccentricity, theatricality, squabbles and bad food; a very English admixture and one that seems to have sustained the Garrick through its erratic early years. It was a disputatious, and often disagreeable, place in the Victorian era. Not so today; through the course of this century it has gradually been acquiring the status of one of the most respectable, popular (there is a very long waiting list) and convivial of London's great gentlemen's clubs. There is still the occasional row, as when Bernard Levin was blackballed. The members tend to be politicians, civil servants, journalists, and—supremely—lawyers: solicitors, barristers and judges. (The club is situated in Garrick Street—the street was named after the club, not vice versa—in the Covent Garden area and is nearer to the Inns of Court than the many clubs in the St James area.) There are fewer actors these days; younger actors tend to gravitate to the Groucho Club, very different from the Garrick.

Given that the club is now much used by senior Tory politicians, it has slowly been acquiring something of an establishment aura. Jeremy Paxman, in his book *Friends in High Places*, recounts that Malcolm Turnbull, the Australian lawyer who fought the *Spycatcher* case through the courts, claimed to have gathered useful intelligence about the tactics of the then Attorney-General, Lord Havers, because he was in the habit of discussing the case in the urinals of the Garrick.

The Garrick's position at the centre of the English firmament was confirmed for me when I heard Sir Ralf Dahrendorf, that great ornament of English academic life, addressing a seminar in Edinburgh on the future of Europe. He said that the English had been quite philosophical about waiting to join the EC, because they really regarded it as a club, and they realised you had to wait to join a club.

Sir Ralf then explained that he had been quite content to bide his time before joining the Garrick. (His moral, incidentally, was that other countries could not afford to be so patient; he was pressing, with some fervour, for early entry of countries like Poland and Czechoslovakia to the EC.)

The Garrick's newfound status has not been achieved without inducing some backbiting. Frederic Raphael, writing about Graham Greene in the *Sunday Times* after the writer's death in April 1991, included the barbed sentence: "If it is hard to see why he was denied the Nobel, we may thank God that he declined to court the kind of knighthood gained by services to the Garrick bar."

I am being entertained to dinner at the Garrick by Geoffrey Parkhouse, political editor of the *Glasgow Herald*, who may not have been knighted but is certainly a man who has served his time at the Garrick bar. I arrive before him and am directed up the splendid staircase by a porter resplendent in green livery. He asks me, very politely, not to go into the bar but to wait in one of the adjoining rooms. I do so and study the theatrical pictures which adorn every available inch of wall space. Many of them are by John Zoffany, the greatest of all theatrical portraitists.

The Garrick is a large, almost monumental building, but the mellow panelling and the clutter of theatrical memorabilia everywhere speak of good fellowship and intimacy—with just a suggestion of louche shabbiness. The real warmth is maintained not so much by the rich decoration and the theatrical effects, but by the members and staff—as I am to discover.

A smartly attired barman approaches me and invites me into the bar, where he pours me a large whisky. Soon Geoffrey arrives and immediately all is banter. A French waitress offers him her packet of cigarettes because the bar does not stock his favourite brand. Some gently flirtatious badinage ensues. Another of the bar stewards, hearing that I come from Scotland, asks me in all seriousness if I can please arrange some shooting and fishing for him.

We proceed downstairs and into the dining room. Unlike most London clubs, the Garrick can be as lively at night as it is at lunchtime. The convention is that those sitting at the long table in the middle of the dining room should speak to their neighbours, even though they may not know them.

Round the room are smaller tables, where there are a few lady guests, sprinkled—it has to be said—somewhat forlornly in this undoubtedly male ambience. At one table a Cabinet minister, John Wakeham, is dining with his son and a senior civil servant. Geoffrey introduces us and then we take our places at the long table.

As the evening progresses, I get to know the member on my left, a barrister called Michael Rich. A most affable man, he laughs uproariously at my bad joke when we are introduced: "Rich by name, rich by nature."

The food is excellent, if unadventurous. Geoffrey says it has improved enormously since the club started taking on French staff to prepare and serve it. "They know far more about food than any of us do," he says. But the conversation flows so vigorously that food is a secondary consideration to the table talk.

Michael Rich adeptly sidesteps my somewhat ponderous questioning about the condition of England, saying that he prefers to think in terms of the United Kingdom rather than just England. I find this hard to believe, but—able barrister that he is—he puts up a persuasive case. Then he and Geoffrey and myself become involved in a debate, at once amiable and quite heated, about alleged war criminals in England and whether they should still be prosecuted. A consensus is eventually reached, that they should not—but it is reached on pragmatic rather than moral grounds, a very English conclusion.

Slowly the guests begin to leave. We are invited across to the table of John Bromley, a man who used to be famous, or notorious, depending on your point of view, for the hard bargains he drove with the English football authorities on the televising of the sport when he was with ITV.

Like Michael Rich, he possesses a disarming affability. He now runs his own company, called Television Sport and Leisure Ltd; his guest is Michael Humphrey, who runs a sports marketing company. The talk is now all about the forthcoming rugby world cup, but then it takes on a more gossipy note. The final discussion centres on the pre-television career of Dickie Davies, the former sports presenter. Not quite what I'd expected at the Garrick; but then television, and its personalities and subculture, have perhaps replaced literature in the English pantheon of interests. For literary giants, substitute television personalities . . . .

The Commentators

Cricket and football are the great English sports. Football has become hyper-professional, over-commercialised, subject to constant hype and spurious over-promotion. Gazza is the supreme, unfortunate, example of this tendency. Cricket, on the other hand, retains at least some dignity. Lord Mancroft once said that the English, not being a spiritual people, invented cricket to give themselves some conception of eternity.

The first cricket Test to be broadcast in full was the Lord's Test of 1948 (England v. Australia) but *Test Match Special*—the radio programme which provided all-day ball-by-ball commentaries, and was to become one of contemporary England's most endearing institutions, was not born till 1957.

Some of England's best-loved sports broadcasters then proceeded to make the programme their own—John Arlott and Brian "Johners" Johnston in particular. Over the years, the actual cricket slowly began to take second place to the chatter. This trend delighted the growing number of listeners who were not obsessed with cricket. Indeed, some evidently yearned for rain—which comes frequently enough in English summers—so that they could enjoy the commentators' prattle, uninterrupted by anything as prosaic as an actual description of the play. But at the same time this trend irritated the true aficionados, people like Caldicott and Charters, the cricket buffs (and buffers) played with such consummate comic zest by Naunton Wayne and Basil Radford in Alfred Hitchcock's finest film, *The Lady Vanishes*.

TMS was slowly developing a dual personality. John Arlott from Hampshire and Don "The Alderman" Mosey from Yorkshire were the serious exponents of dedicated, almost dour, description of the play; Brian Johnston and Henry "Blowers" Blofeld were more light-hearted, not to say downright frivolous. They were the prattlers, but they elevated prattle to an art form.

Brian Johnston, who was once sacked by BBC TV for being too jokey, was given to discussing the plot—if it can be thus designated—of *Neighbours* at great length, and also to delivering supposedly unintentional double entendres. He told me in 1990 that despite the prattle about teacakes and *Neighbours* and just about everything else under the sun, he had not missed a ball yet. "Anyway, you can't just shut up. Cricket is a very slow game, and it can take a fast bowler a minute between balls. You have to fill in. And yes, the housewives—terrible word, I mean the ladies—they do love it when it rains. They prefer non-stop chat to the cricket. Sometimes I don't blame them either. I love cricket, I go every day expecting to see the best day's cricket ever, but it is getting too grim. These days, you rarely see cricketers smile."

But when Johnston is around, the characteristic jokiness is never far away. "Did you hear about the famous time I said: 'The bowler's Holding, the batsman's Willey?' Or the time when the batsman was badly hit fifth ball? Eventually he recovered and I said: 'Yes, he's going to go on batting. He's got one ball left!'"

Dear Country

Yet in my opinion the supreme prattler was always Henry Blofeld. His counterpoints with that great fast bowler of the 1950s and 1960s, Fred "Fiery Fred" Trueman, a gruff, gritty Yorkshireman if ever there was one, were particularly entertaining, full of improvised passages for the connoisseur. But if Henry Blofeld could blether with fluent and sublime inconsequence—he could describe a piece of litter blowing across Trent Bridge as if he were reading a translation of a poem by Baudelaire—he could also commentate, most professionally, and with great insight and knowledge, on the actual cricket.

Henry was first taken to Lord's, his favourite ground, when he was eight, to watch the Monday play in the aforementioned 1948 Test against the Aussies. He sat with his parents and ate two punnets of strawberries, one in the morning, one in the afternoon. He can still recall the taste of those strawberries, picked from a small field at Hoveton in Norfolk. More to the point, he can still recall the cricket. He was hooked.

Henry Blofeld, now fifty-one, belongs to an ancient Norfolk family. His father was a great friend of Ian Fleming, the inventor of James Bond. The nastiest, and thus the best, villain in the Bond books is called Blofeld, a joke directed at Henry's father.

He was educated at Eton, where he became the outstanding cricketer of his day: he was, by all accounts, an elegant wicketkeeper and a distinguished opening bat. He was precocious enough to play for Eton against Harrow at Lord's when he was only fifteen (Eton won by 38 runs). He would assuredly have become the last Old Etonian to play for England had he not, at the age of seventeen, suffered a quite hideous accident. He was on his bicycle and came off worse after an argument with a bus—so much worse that he was unconscious for thirty-eight days, and went through no fewer than fourteen brain operations. He is thus lucky to be alive; but a glittering cricket career was denied him, though he did win his Blue at Cambridge before finally giving up.

He was sent down from Cambridge, and after various adventures he became, almost inevitably, a journalist. He has written several books: he once wrote one in eight days, and if this suggests that he is slapdash or superficial, you should not be deceived. He is actually a most graceful and thoughtful writer, as shown for example by the superb passage describing Georgetown, Guyana, in his latest book, *On the Edge of My Seat*.

Henry Blofeld was with *Test Match Special* for seventeen years. He eventually quit, at the end of 1990, to join BSkyB.

"One reason, my dear old thing, was money: the BBC are not good payers, and BSkyB offered me so much that I simply had to leave."

Another reason was his instinct that *TMS* was at last losing its magic. For some time its future had been in doubt; and Brian Johnston, its most loved and longstanding master, was nearing eighty. Also, Don Mosey wrote to Henry Blofeld warning him that he was bringing out a book—predictably called *The Alderman's Tale*—in which he would be saying one or two things which might change the atmosphere in the commentary box.

In the event, Mosey's book was pretty innocuous. He did recall how he had once "asked Henry Blofeld, after a particularly over-the-top performance, 'Have you ever wondered what listeners in Oswaldwhistle and Cleckheaton think about your style of commentary?' And Henry replied, 'My dear old thing' (of course). 'No, should I?'"

Mosey adds that he had often asked himself if listeners in Bognor Regis and Cheltenham Spa could accept his north country idiom. He had told Henry that he should care about what ALL the listeners were thinking.

Then Mosey says, referring back to the Blofeld incident, that this was an example of where *TMS* had tended to lose its way. "We have become far too self-satisfied and self-indulgent."

That is about the extent of Mosey's criticism of Henry Blofeld, though he does comment that to have Henry "my-dear-old-thinging" around Headingley at a Roses Match (Yorkshire v. Lancashire) was as absurdly anachronistic as appointing George Best to introduce *Songs of Praise*.

Surprisingly, given the tenor of this book, Mosey tells a story that seems to sum up the silly, frivolous side of *TMS* at its best. When rain had yet again stopped play in a Test Match, David

Dear Country

Lloyd talked about his new garden, which included a fishpond. Fred Trueman had warned him to watch out for herons. David Lloyd had then "with just the right touch of pathos" responded: "We don't get a right lot of herons in the middle of Accrington, Fred."

Mosey's book is an entertaining read, crammed with sporting anecdotes. A theme running through it, however, is resentment of home county, public school types. This is another variation on England's north-south divide. Indeed, the very first sentences of the book read: "It seems to be fashionable in some quarters to sneer at any story of a northerner who emerges from humble origins to fashion some sort of better life for himself. It may, therefore, come as a surprise to the sneerers to learn that we enjoy a cliché of our own—to look down our nose at a fair number in the effete south who seem to us to achieve success through influence and string-pulling rather than honest toil."

But by the time that *The Alderman's Tale* came out, in the late summer of 1991, Henry Blofeld was well established with BSkyB, having commentated on the England–West Indies Test series for them.

Henry is a large, jovial figure. He sports loud shirts and bow ties. He used to be a great man for the clubs and discos, but he is gradually settling down. (He recently married for the third time: his wife, Bitten, is a Swede.) He has been in numerous scrapes; he was once imprisoned in New York. As with many naturally funny men, there is a tinge of melancholy about him. He is aware that he is slowing down. "I used to think the day started at ten at night. Now I'm just about ready to retire at ten. You still have fun as you get older, but it is more responsible fun."

He genuinely loves five-day cricket—the slow tensions, the suspense, the swings of fortune—just as he detests one-day cricket, though he accepts that it has become a necessary evil. "But you usually only need turn up for the last hour."

Test cricket, he thinks has become too professional. "There is too much coaching, too much shouting at the players. I don't like to see a coach making players run round a track."

Late in 1991, the BBC announced that all threats to *TMS* had been removed, and that it would continue as before. But without Henry Blofeld, it cannot continue as before. It will never be quite so agreeable and idiosyncratic. It will be bereft of that most pleasing of characteristics, charm.

CHAPTER TEN

BELLS AND BANDS

Ashbourne—Manchester

I drove along the M62 from Langley, towards Leeds, and turned off just as the great motorway was beginning its climb up the moors. I then drove down through Delph and Saddleworth and Stalybridge to Glossop; past old mills, through dirty, steep country, past the filthiest sheep I've ever seen, past grim, truncated terraces of houses left on grimy hillsides. This was a land that should have been beautiful, but looked scarred and forsaken; and it also looked as if it needed a good scrub.

I was heading towards Ashbourne in Derbyshire, because it is more or less in the middle of England. When I arrived the town seemed beset by gridlock, like so many English towns these days. I eventually got parked and went to the post office for some stamps. The man who sold them to me recommended that I should visit the parish church of St Oswald. This was completely unsolicited advice, but he was so enthusiastic that I followed his directions.

As I approached the church, the bells were ringing, as if

Dear Country

summoning me, and endorsing the post office man's suggestion. It turned out that the churchfolk were celebrating the 750th anniversary of St Oswald's. A group of them were milling around the nave, arranging an informal exhibition. At the door stood the verger, who told me categorically that St Oswald's was the finest parish church in all England. He added that its brass consecration plate was the oldest brass in England.

I was more interested in the bellringers, who were busy at work in the nave, not the belfry. The verger explained that the belfry was no longer used because its masonry was in a dangerous state. But he was worried about the bellropes, which were seventy-five feet long. He said that one of the bells weighed three-quarters of a ton, and he was concerned about whiplash if the ringer lost his grip.

When the ringing ceased, I chatted with the ringer of the tenor bell—the very heavy one which the verger had mentioned. He told me that the bells were rung to invite people to worship on Sundays, morning and evening. There was also a practice once a week; and of course they were rung at weddings and funerals. He showed me the leather muffles that could be attached to the bell clappers, so that the sound could be either half-deadened, or almost completely obliterated.

I said I didn't see much point in bellringing if there was no sound; but full muffles were evidently used only when the monarch died. Half-muffles were used for funerals, on Remembrance Sunday and for ringing out the Old Year. He told me that he and his colleagues sometimes rang a peel, which involved at least 5,040 changes, and took a good three hours.

Both the terminology and the mathematics of change-ringing are arcane. Change-ringing requires the ringers to weave their bells among each other, according to predetermined sequences which have names such as Plain Bob Minimus or Oswald Delight Minor. These mathematical sequences can be extremely complicated, or so it seemed to me as the ringer patiently talked me through them.

I sometimes get the impression that the English can take something essentially simple, like the game of cricket or the ringing of bells, and transform it into something recondite, which in turn creates a kind of freemasonry for the initiated.

At St Oswald's there were eight bells, cast by William Dobson of Downham Market. (Four or more bells are needed for proper circle change-ringing.) In most other countries, carillons or automated chimes are used; manual ringing continues to flourish in England. Yet like many other apparently quintessential English customs—such as maypole dancing—the bellringing that is practised now is really a sanitised version reinvented by the Victorians. Earlier, bellringing was as much a secular as a religious activity and belfries were often regarded as places of sin, where booze-ups and fornication and other related depravity took place.

I stayed overnight in Ashbourne and the next morning I journeyed the short distance east to Breadsall, a village a few miles to the north of Derby which sits at the exact centre of England. (I am indebted to the geographer Dr Robert Rogerson for this information.)

Breadsall turned out to be the leafy, quiet, insulated kind of village, full of prosperous private houses and bereft of public houses, which is to be found somewhere not too far from most English cities. This kind of village is not genuinely bucolic. Rather it is a redoubt for short-distance commuters.

Hedges were being trimmed, gardens were being watered. It was Sunday morning, and a few modest cars were parked outside the church. Occasionally the peace was disturbed by more expensive cars moving rather too fast up the hill past the church. I gather that the villagers of Breadsall were specially congratulated by the enumerators of the 1991 National Census for their charm and helpfulness. It appeared to be that kind of place; almost too good to be true.

I moved on up the hill, and looked around. The landscape was rich and green though there were one or two bright yellow fields of oilseed rape. The woodlands were lovely and deeply English: natural broadleafed trees scattered in copses and spinneys, and no forests. The sound accompaniment came from a distant cuckoo and the inevitable throb of traffic (this from the busy A38, a mile or so away). The odd jogger and cyclist moved stealthily through this sylvan landscape—again, I noticed an absence of walkers—and the occasional executive car roared past.

Then, looking to the east, I noticed what seemed to be a dump of sand in a sloping field. As I looked more closely, three gaudily coloured figures hove into view. Golfers, walking past a bunker.

Sure enough, further up the road I came to the Breadsall Priory Hotel Golf and Country Club. The drive and car park were thick with BMWs (Bad Man's Wagons, as they are known in some quarters), Mercs and Volvos. Parked outside the hotel reception area was yet another BMW; inside it a woman was yapping into her carphone.

The golfers looked intense and glum, despite their garish clothes; they obviously took their pastime very seriously. I thought of the relatively few cars down the road at the church, and the admittedly banal thought occurred: Is golf the new religion of England? The Tory Party at play, rather than at prayer, in these secular, leisure-driven times?

Certainly the march of the golfer is concerning English conservationists. In the Midlands—and I was deep in the Midlands that Sunday morning—there are currently 227 golf courses. But it is reckoned that another 150—yes, 150—will be needed to meet the demands of frustrated Midlands golfers by the year 2000. If all the current planning applications for new golf courses in England—and 1,400 are on the table—are granted, they would cover an area of land the size of the Isle of Wight.

In a sense, golf courses protect the landscape. But they also destroy it. I recalled Graham Greene's *aperçu*: "A crematorium garden resembles a real garden about as much as a golf links resembles a genuine landscape."

Back in Ashbourne, I wandered into the Beresford Arms Hotel for a mid-afternoon pint of Marston's Pedigree bitter. Here, in the big lounge, there was an extraordinary scene. A three-piece combo—sax, electric guitar and keyboard—was belting out MOR standards with great brio. But the lugubrious audience consisted of a grumpy-looking man reading the *Sunday Times*, a trio talking with sullen intensity in a corner, and the woman behind the bar. Perhaps everybody else in Ashbourne had better things to do, but there was something spooky about the way the musicians were being ignored. I felt sorry for them; they were giving all they had, and on effort alone they deserved a bigger and more responsive audience.

As I strolled through the little country town that afternoon, I was conscious of noise. Not the sound of the combo, although that was still vaguely resonating in my head; not the mellow, plangent sound of church bells; not the eternal sweetness of birdsong. No, the noise was the noise of the traffic, grinding its way slowly through the narrow streets in a laborious, frustrated, overheated procession; and also the distant whine of motor bikes, racing on a nearby track. Noise is the worst pollutant in many English towns.

Early the next day, Bank Holiday Monday, I was in Manchester for the Whit Walks, which had been described to me by the Rev. Ian Johnson, half jokingly, as a "ritual of appalling proportions".

The walks used to be a major event in Manchester's calendar—in the immediate post-war years as many as 40,000 people took part—but in the 1970s interest dwindled and the city's Anglican leaders considered abandoning them. But in the last few years there has been something of a revival.

As I arrived at Cross St, just up from Albert Square, I could hear in the distance the aggressive beat of a big drum. In Scotland this would have signified an Orange Walk, an event often attended by menace and foreboding, but the mood of the Whit Walks was very different: gentle, happy, and a pleasing mix of the secular and the liturgical.

A few somewhat sheepish-looking clerics led the walkers towards Albert Square where there was to be a short service. Then came pageants presented by seventeen separate parishes. Some paraded beautiful religious banners; others featured flower girls, some of them so young they could hardly walk, in lovingly prepared outfits. Then there were the bands. I counted eleven in all, with the Micklehurst Brass Band the pick of the bunch.

As the walkers and musicians passed by, I noticed that the only people who looked embarrassed, who looked as if they wished they were somewhere else, were the clergy. Some of them—including the Rev. Ian Johnson, who marched past carrying an orange balloon—entered into the spirit of the occasion, but others looked distinctly unhappy.

There must have been between 3,000 and 4,000 taking part. When everyone had assembled in Albert Square, in front of Alfred Waterhouse's magnificent Town Hall, the Bishop of Hulme urged the walkers to come forward—and to be quiet. Few paid any attention. The secular aspect of the occasion was now to the fore. Some men were drinking beer from cans, and children were clamouring for ice cream. Whistles were being blown and balloons were popping. Union Jacks were being purchased from vendors at a great rate. The bishop's pleas for quiet went unheeded.

Then, in a flash of crimson, the small, portly figure of George Chadwick, the Lord Mayor, could be seen scurrying round the fringes of the crowd, and then pressing his way through the throng to join the bishop. The service could now begin. As it was Manchester, it started to rain at this point; Union Jack umbrellas opened up all over the square. But it proved to be just a thin drizzle.

The brief service concluded with a spirited singing of the national anthem—the only point at which most of those in the square joined in. Then the parade proper was underway, led by the bechained Lord Mayor, resplendent in his red coat, and the bishop.

Up through narrow streets towards the Arndale Centre they went, and on down the shallow hill to Manchester Cathedral, where a second, more formal service was to take place. The crowds were now lining the streets four or five deep; onlookers were peering from every deck of the Arndale multi-storey car park. Each band was loudly cheered as it passed by; thousands of Union Jacks were waved; and the Lord Mayor appeared to be enjoying himself hugely at the head of the procession.

I did not stay for the second service; instead I returned to Albert Square, through streets now thronged with happy people. There was a peculiar innocence in the air; the atmosphere was somehow that of the '50s rather than the '90s. The pubs were thronged to the point of spilling out into the streets; but there was no menace or unpleasantness. Mind you, the day was young.

Albert Square, was now, alas, filthy. Litter was everywhere. A ring of lager cans surrounded the Albert Memorial. The Whit Walks may have cheered Bank Holiday Manchester up; they certainly had not cleaned it up.

Manchester was without doubt the dirtiest place I visited in England. Of course, the downside of Manchester is not confined to filth in the streets. There are racial tensions; there is a serious drugs problem. Statistical evidence suggests, however, that Manchester is less violent than England's other big cities; and the people are very friendly, if excessively loquacious.

Furthermore, Manchester is making far-sighted efforts to give itself an efficient transport infrastructure. There was serious traffic congestion in the city centre when I was there—but that was because the streets were being ripped up for the new Metrolink development. This "state of the art" rapid transport system—a combination of light trains and trams—is being developed by both the public and private sectors at a cost of £150 million.

Manchester, unlike London, is surrounded by an extensive network of motorways. At times this network is overstretched, but it is by no means permanently jammed. The main north-south motorway, the M6, bypasses the conurbation to the west; the main east-west motorway, the M62, loops round the western and northern fringes of Manchester itself. In addition the city is served by the M56, the A57(M), the M61, the M63, the M66, the M67, the A627(M) and the M602. All this amounts to well over 250 miles of motorway in the immediate environs of the city.

Even more impressive is the locally-owned Manchester Airport, which for some time has been the fastest-growing international passenger airport in Europe. An estimated 25 million passengers per year will be using it by 2000; a second international terminal is now being built. In 1993 a high-speed dedicated rail link from the airport to the city centre will be operational; the journey time will be only twelve minutes.

This brief summary indicates that Manchester is moving well ahead of London (and Birmingham) in addressing its transport problems. It is developing an integrated transport system that is user-friendly.

The city is already England's second financial centre, boasting more than seventy five foreign banks. It also possesses a huge student population—the largest of any city in Europe, according to the city's PR people—and has recently established itself as an innovative music centre. More traditional music will soon have a superb context; the Hallé Orchestra is to be housed in a grand new £90 million concert hall. The British Council headquarters are to be sited in Manchester. The Manchester Ship Canal Company is imaginatively regenerating the upper canalside reaches.

Manchester has some splendid Victorian architecture, which gives its town centre great dignity and gravitas. It has no grand boulevards (never a feature of Victorian urban design, as Peter Hennessy has noted) but it does boast the superb town hall, already mentioned. It also affords relatively easy access to an abundant variety of country: from the Lake District to the dales of west Yorkshire; from the Peak District to green and gentle Cheshire. And of course there is the seaside: the very different resorts of Southport, Lytham, Blackpool and Morecambe are all only an hour or so away.

Another plus for Manchester is that it possesses the world's most famous, and glamorous, football team, Manchester United.

United have had a bad spell and have not in fact won the English League championship since the halcyon, giddy era of George Best and Denis Law and that most gracious and gentlemanly of English footballers, Bobby Charlton. (How different he was, and is, from his fellow Geordie, Gazza.) This galaxy of talent was orchestrated by a shrewd Scots manager, Sir Matt Busby. Now another Scot, Alex Ferguson, a man I have known for a long time and regard as the deepest thinker about football I have ever met, is slowly but surely guiding Man U back to their rightful place—at the top.

English football was in disgrace in the late 1980s, after the Heysel débâcle which so tarnished the good name of Liverpool FC. Manchester United were allowed back into Europe in 1990-91 and they immediately won the Cup Winners' Cup, beating Barcelona in the Rotterdam final, thanks to a marvellous goal from the Welshman Mark Hughes and a finely judged tactical performance devised by Ferguson. But much more important was the fact that the thousands of English supporters in Rotterdam behaved in exemplary fashion; they were indeed magnificent ambassadors for their team and its city. When I was in Manchester there was still a buzz and a glow from this achievement; this had been English football's proudest night for quite some time, and certainly a much more dignified and positive occasion than the absurd "tears of Gazza" episode which elicited so much nonsensical hype as the English national team bowed out of the World Cup the previous summer.

If Greater Manchester has a difficulty at present, it lies in what image of itself it wishes to project. It is richer in industrial history than anywhere else in the world. Its network of canals is in itself a magnificent testament to the engineering genius of some of the great industrial pioneers of the late eighteenth century. The city can claim to be the world's outstanding urban prototype, in that it was the first great factory city created in the western world. This is Manchester's real heritage, but how should it be presented?

In 1701 the city's population was 10,000. A century later it was 70,000, and fifty years after that it had risen to 300,000. The industrial revolution was an explosion of energy and invention, of economic drive and engineering innovation—but it left in its wake a series of social horror stories, attendant on the creation of the world's first genuine proletariat.

Friedrich Engels, who collaborated with Karl Marx in the theoretical development of modern communism, worked in Manchester (as an employer rather than an employee) through the middle years of the nineteenth century. His book, *The Condition of the Working Classes in England in 1844*, with its terrible account of the slums of Manchester and its descriptions of "hollowed-eyed ghosts", the zombies who toiled for grotesquely long hours in the city's factories, contains the most powerful indictment of the conditions spawned by the revolution. It is a peculiar book, inaccurate and in some aspects downright silly; and as a sociological critique it leaves much to be desired. But it is driven by an almost poetic horror, and Engels was a much more sympathetic, much more human writer than his collaborator Marx.

Why the industrial revolution did not bring in its wake a more orthodox political revolution is one of the more pertinent questions of English political and social history; but the English have a penchant for avoiding violent upheavals by the judicious implementation of last-minute reform. The response to the industrial revolution, slow and stuttering as it was, is the tale of many honorable efforts.

How then, should all this—perhaps the most intensely experienced and acutely localised passage of social history the world has ever known—how should it all be purveyed today? Obviously it must not be prettified or petrified, over-commercialised or over-packaged. Nor, however, should it be ignored. I suspect that those who are pushing Manchester's bid for the 2000 Olympics will be embarrassed by the L. S. Lowry syndrome, the persistent images of defeated men wearing cloth caps, and satanic mills belching smoke. But I hope they do not anaesthetise the city too much, and present it as an American-style twenty-first-century megacity. I hope they will take as much pride in Manchester's problematic past as in its undoubted potential.

I discussed the strategy for the bid with Mike Cuerden, a consultant who will soon be working on it full-time. I met him in a huge empty office suite in Bridgwater House, round the corner from the Palace Theatre. When I walked in, the place was literally deserted—just row upon row of empty desks. Eventually a girl appeared, and then Mike himself. But it will be a different picture as the momentum builds up toward decision day, in Monaco in September 1993.

Manchester has been over the course once already. Its bid for the 1996 games was creditable, though it fell far short of success. If mistakes were made, so was considerable progress. The effort second-time around will be stronger and more sophisticated. Certainly the British Olympic Committee who decided by twenty-eight votes to five that Manchester rather than London should mount the British bid for the 2000 games, seem to have regarded the 1996 bid as a useful "dry run" rather than a flop.

The strategy will be to emphasise the region, rather than just the city. Thus centres like Chester will be involved as well as Greater Manchester. The competition is not yet known, but it looks like including Beijing, Sydney, Berlin, Milan, Brasilia and possibly Istanbul. But sporting contacts have told me that all these cities—and Manchester—will almost certainly fall by the wayside if a South African city makes a coherent bid.

Manchester does not as yet possess an Olympic Stadium, let alone an Olympic village. But a more than adequate site has been earmarked, near the Barton Aerodrome at Eccles, where more than 1,000 acres are available less than five miles from the city centre. If Manchester does get the green light in 1993, work will start immediately.

Whether Manchester succeeds or not, the bid will have credibility. It will also do much to enhance Manchester's burgeoning status as England's second city and will—more significantly—be a test of England's social, cultural and political unity. Theoretically the bid is not Manchester's but Britain's. I am sure that Scotland and Wales and English regions such as the North-east and the Midlands, will wish Manchester well and do what they can in support.

What will be interesting will be the extent to which London backs the bid. As Mike Cuerden says: "We want to get the phrase Manchester 2000 into the national vocabulary." I'm not sure that "Manchester 2000" will enter the London vocabulary without sticking in the metropolitan throat.

I chatted about Manchester's renaissance with Katie Jones, a producer with Granada Television. Katie is a Londoner, but a Manchester convert. She stressed to me that London can no longer claim the cultural monopoly that it did, all too easily, ten years ago.

"I'd say there is probably a greater diversity of cultural experience now on offer in Manchester than in London," she said. "And here it's less exclusive, it's much cheaper—and you don't have the terrible hassle of getting to it. Once you get out of London, you quickly realise that you can enjoy a better lifestyle—but try telling that to Londoners. Most Londoners still consider the rest of England to be a cultural backwater." She said she found it difficult to persuade her London friends to come to Manchester, even for a short visit.

Katie said that part and parcel of Manchester's cultural maturing was a new civic self-confidence. It was also developing socially, without any excessive yuppification. Many areas were obviously changing for the better—but not at the expense of the traditional residents, as in London's Docklands. (Manchester has its docklands developments too, but not on the grotesque and insensitive scale of those in London.) And the areas which catered for Manchester's huge transient population had also improved, and become internationalised.

We had lunch in a wine bar in West Didsbury—in itself, I suppose, an example of the changing nature of Manchester— and then I set off for a long walk round the western fringes of the city. I was aiming for Worsley, where the Duke of Bridgewater started the canal system that was so crucial to the industrial revolution. I also wanted to look at the proposed Barton site for the Olympics, but somehow I managed to miss it.

My slightly wayward route first took me along the Wilmslow Road, before I struck out to the west. This thoroughfare was without doubt the filthiest I have ever come across anywhere. It is one of Manchester's main arteries, leading from the city centre directly to some fatcat suburbs in the south of Greater Manchester; it goes past the university, and near, but not through, the notorious areas of Hulme and Moss Side. It is a lively street, filled with a diversity of shops and, at its southern end, a great number of restaurants and small hotels. It is thus by no means the kind of degraded drag that you might expect to find in a ghetto area.

But as I walked along it I found myself literally ankle deep in litter. The debris was thick on the ground—not just in the gutters but right across the pavements. Only the street itself was comparatively clean, but even on it enough trash was blowing around to constitute a traffic hazard. Other people were wading through the mess, apparently unconcerned.

After a long walk I found myself in Eccles, an area of run-down gentility, characterised as much as anything else by its multiplicity of pubs. I popped into the TU unemployment centre, for I was conscious that—litter apart—I was forming a very positive view of Greater Manchester; and yet I was aware that the conurbation had its downbeat side, not least because of its unemployment rate of 15 per cent.

Inside the centre I found no Englishmen, but an articulate compatriot, Tommy McIntyre, and an equally articulate Irishman, Sean Keeley. Both had been unemployed for some time. They told me about the North-west People's March for Jobs, from Manchester to Liverpool, which had been organised to mark the tenth anniversary of the great People's March to London of 1981.

The 1991 March was starting at Manchester Town Hall in two days' time. I was to be in Cheshire and Staffordshire then, but we agreed that I could join the march later, on the Wigan–Skelmersdale stretch. I wished them well, and resumed my own mini-march towards Worsley. I was tired as I approached the place, on a long, straight path alongside the Bridgewater Canal. Suddenly I thought I was hallucinating. The canal had started to change colour—from a dark sludgy grey to a vivid orange. It was an eerie sensation; it was as if I was on some exotic 1960s-style trip, when all I had indulged in was a modest amount of alcohol several hours earlier.

I was told later that there remain great deposits of iron ore from the old mine workings around Worsley, and this accounts for the canal's peculiar change of colour.

I liked Worsley, a quiet place, very much part of Greater Manchester yet discrete, a place that proved difficult to categorise: neither town nor village nor suburb nor outskirt. For one of the great cradles of industrialisation, it had a semi-rustic air; here, once again, was evidence of the English drive to bring the country to the town rather than vice versa. It boasted a bucolic-looking green where once there were great manufacturing shops and workplaces. Hereabouts, where the canal passed the green, it was all rather prettified—despite the garish colour of the water—with a number of brightly-painted canal boats and the church of St Mark's just visible beyond the trees.

Some of the men who used to work here evidently infuriated the great engineering Duke of Bridgewater by being persistently late for work after lunch. Their explanation was that they could hear the clock strike twelve, but not one. The duke promptly arranged for it to strike thirteen times at one o'clock; and the clock of St Mark's evidently does so to this day.

I went to investigate St Mark's; a handsome enough church, so far as I could judge from the outside. But it was shut—the only church I had tried to get into that was locked up. It occupied an embattled site, with the busy M62 on one side and the equally busy A572 and A575 squeezing past on two other sides.

A few yards from St Mark's is the entrance to an extraordinary network of underground canals that was built by the duke and his right-hand man, James Brindley, England's greatest-ever engineer, a self-taught country boy who became a canal-builder of superlative genius, creating almost 400 miles of waterways without one written calculation or a single drawing.

The Worsley–Manchester canal was the first great industrial canal in England, and the crucial one; the cheap coal that came from the mines of Worsley to Manchester allowed the great explosion of factory-building that really got the industrial revolution going. This overground canal linked up with the forty-six miles of subterranean canals, on four different levels, that were driven through the duke's Worsley coalfields.

Although these underground canals were abandoned long ago (the mines themselves more recently) I wondered why no entrepreneur had thought to open them up. That would be a most unusual, not to say darkly exciting, tourist attraction—and a heritage facility of integrity, a robust reminder of the achievements of industrialisation, of the engineering triumphs that led to enormous national prosperity, and at the same time to untold misery for thousands upon thousands of exploited workers, many of them little children.

Here, as nowhere else in England, a country rich in history, is history that is at once noble and tragic, at once thrilling and rebarbative.

CHAPTER ELEVEN

FOX ON THE LINE

Crewe—Stoke

It used to be difficult to find someone in England who had never changed trains at Crewe. Nowadays many young English people do not even associate Crewe with the railway—a symptom of the decline in England's use of the transport system it gave to the world. Crewe was for many years the archetypal railway junction, and it remains an exceptionally busy station. It survived the Beeching butchery of the 1960s unscathed and today it remains at the nucleus of a great radius of lines. The main west coast Carlisle–Euston line runs through Crewe; other lines peel off from the station to Manchester, Derby, Chester and Shrewsbury. A little to the north, the Liverpool line branches off; and a little to the south, the Wolverhampton line branches off. This pattern of lines radiating from Crewe was completed in 1858, and has thus remained intact for 133 years.

Crewe itself is a neat, workmanlike town, full of redbrick terraces. It did not exist 150 years ago, but by 1879 its population had risen to 24,000. The first small station was built in the 1840s; it was rebuilt in 1863, and significantly extended in 1906.

Then in the summer of 1985 the station was closed for seven weeks and the entire track layout and signalling system was remodelled at a cost of more than £14 million. The number of points and crossings was greatly reduced; trains could now pass through the station at 80 m.p.h. instead of 20 m.p.h. Most of the old manual signalboxes were replaced by a new signalling centre to the north of the station, a development that was not altogether welcomed by the signalmen. The station now covers twenty-six acres. There are five through platforms and seven bay (dead end) platforms. Around 400 trains pass through Crewe on an average weekday, including 145 InterCity trains (thirty of which do not stop) and 135 local passenger trains. Most freight trains avoid the station for there are "independent" lines bypassing it to the huge Basford Hall marshalling yard immediately to the south, where about 130 trains are processed every twenty-four hours, many of them by night.

I spent a full day at the station and its adjacent marshalling yard, chatting to the staff. To my surprise, I found morale generally high. Among the older railmen there was agreement that the 1960s and 1970s had been an appalling time for them, with the end of steam and the bitterness engendered by the many redundancies of the Beeching era.

One driver of thirty-seven years' experience said that it used to be much harder work—but more interesting. Boredom had become a serious problem; the driver sat in his cab, alone and insulated from all around him: concentration could be difficult. I asked what had been worst about the old days. "The fog," he said. "No doubt about it, the fog. Particularly in the London and Wigan areas. You couldn't see the signals, you couldn't see anything. The air has been cleaned up no end."

At the marshalling yard I heard more stories about the bad old days. A wagon, or even an entire train, could be stuck in a siding for days and no-one would realise that it had gone missing. A train would turn up and would be abandoned in a siding; you had to look at the labels on the wagons to see which train it was; sometimes there were no labels on the wagons. All that changed with TOPS—the computerised Total Operations Processing System, which was introduced in the mid-'70s. This records every single wagon on the entire network; where it is, where it's destined for, what's in it.

One driver at the Basford Hall yard told me that in the 1960s a driver would sometimes sign on, then sit in his loco all day doing absolutely nothing, then sign off and go home. Some drivers refused to acknowledge the very existence of signalmen; others would refuse to let firemen onto their engine unless everything was precisely as regulated in the rulebook. "Where's your brush?" he had heard another driver demand of a fireman. The fireman had no brush; he was not allowed onto the engine; the train did not leave the station. In that era there had been something tantamount to industrial anarchy; now there was much more co-operation and teamwork.

I also heard several tales of encounters with animals. All drivers dread hitting someone on the line, but I was told that trespassing was not too serious a problem, although about 100 trespassers are killed on the railways each year. But drivers hit animals with some regularity. This can be tragic—in Scotland a cow on the main Glasgow–Edinburgh line caused an extremely serious accident in which a train was derailed and thirteen people were killed in 1984. Or messy—I was told the smell from a burnt carcass, dragged along under the train, was unspeakably vile. Or just plain comic.

One driver recalled how he'd once hit a huge bull. He thought he was going to hit it head-on, but at the last moment the bull veered off to the side of the track. Nonetheless the engine gave the animal a great dunt. The driver was amazed that the bull survived; but not only did it survive, he saw it bolting away, clean through—not over—a thick hedgerow. When he had stopped, a hundred yards or so up the track, he moved out of his cab to inspect the damage, if any. He fell headfirst; he had stepped into thin air. The steps at the side of the loco had been sheared away by the impact with the bull.

The mood seemed more upbeat among the drivers than among the signalmen. I had been expecting to find a fairly

Dear Country

disillusioned, grumpy set of workers, and I did not: but the signalmen were distinctly uneasy about some aspects of their job. In the new signalling centre—a bunker-like building, without windows, where three signalmen monitored a huge panel covered with lines and blinking lights—they greatly disliked not being able to see, or even hear, the actual trains (they could just hear the rumble of fast through trains if they strained their ears). They thus felt they had no meaningful link with the great machines, full of people and goods, that were just little blinks on their screen. They felt disembodied, cut off.

Also in the signalling centre was the woman who made the platform announcements—a long way from the platforms—and controlled the televised information screens. The atmosphere inside the centre was informal and friendly, but somewhat claustrophobic.

I also visited two old-fashioned high signalboxes above the railway, or "the road", as all the railmen called it. These were the Salop Goods Junction Box, which controlled the independent freight lines, and the big box at the marshalling yard. In the former the signals were still worked manually, by traditional hand-pulls; and in both of them the signalman could actually survey his domain. The signalman at the freight yard told me he sometimes watched a fox on the sandbank beyond the lines; now it had five cubs.

Later, when I was in the TOPS shed at the yard, chatting to the railman there as he operated his computer screen, I glanced out of the open door across the great expanse of tracks—and there was the fox, loping towards its sandbank. It was a scruffy, rather dingy-looking fox; nonetheless there was something splendidly feral about it as it moved with stealthy purpose across the huge yard in the late afternoon sunlight. A long freight train lumbered slowly past, and the ground shook; but the fox continued its progress, apparently unconcerned.

In the station itself, I saw round the area operating centre, where each and every train's movements are entered on a computer—except for the royal trains, of which there are a surprisingly large number. These are not entered for security reasons.

In the ticket office, which takes almost £2 million a year, the clerk told me he could work for an hour in the early morning before he saw cash; it was all credit cards at that time—businessmen going on InterCity journeys. (About sixty commuters travel the two-hour journey from Crewe to London every morning; most of them, of course, have season tickets.)

Before I left I talked with Jan Glasscock, the area manager, and Mike Addison, the stationmaster, in Mr Glasscock's splendid old-fashioned wood-panelled eyrie above Platform 12. A bowler hat was lying on Mr Glasscock's vast desk; and both gents wore the railway dignitary's three piece suit, complete with watch chain.

Jan Glasscock told me he sometimes worried that the railway was an excessively introverted, inward-looking industry. Certainly I had met several railmen who were the sons, or even grandsons, of railmen; and there was a grand awareness of, almost an obsession with, the past. But the men seemed quite outgoing, not so much suspicious of the outside world at large—which they thought was willy-nilly swinging back to the railway, partly because of the chronic congestion on the roads—as specifically suspicious of politicians and their own senior rail management. (They seemed to have a lot of respect, even affection, for the local management.)

I visited Crewe the day after the Government had announced a major switch in transport policy, with the aim of transferring much freight traffic from rail to road. This was being much discussed by the railmen I met, but discussed with considerable scepticism, not to say cynicism; and, sure enough, just a week later, it was announced that British Rail had been told to mothball hundreds of millions of pounds of planned investment. The new golden age of the railway had lasted precisely eight days.

The railmen I spoke to were slow-spoken, thoughtful men. They saw a strong future for their industry, despite the fickleness and even hostility of politicians. They were happier in their work than I had expected.

A few miles across Cheshire from Crewe, on the other side of the M6 and in the direction of Congleton, is Lower Medhurst Green Farm. Here I met Stuart Yarwood, an intelligent and articulate farmer of thirty-five. He is in partnership with his father and brother. They farm 340 acres on two holdings. There is one hired man on each farm. They have 120 dairy cows and they grow 100 acres of cereals; the other 240 acres are grass. Their milk quota is almost a million litres a year. They sell about sixty heifers at calving each year. The family policy is to grow as much of their cattle's requirements as possible. "We aim for self-sufficiency" is Stuart's motto.

He was milking cows at ten; he was born and bred to the job. He loves it, but he emphasises that it is not a job for people who like to plan carefully. "You cannot really plan anything on the land. It is far, far too unpredictable," he says.

In his view, the farming scene is not as prosperous as it was fifteen years ago. "To get the same quality of life, you simply have to work harder and harder—though I don't do anything like as much physical work as my parents did." He cannot afford to hire another man—he could employ half a man, were that feasible—"but casual labour has dubious reliability," as he puts it.

Although he is a relatively young man, he is already deeply nostalgic for one aspect of farming in the recent past. "The days are gone when two men could do a job in the field and talk to each other. There was good comradeship in the past. Now a man is on his own all the time, probably in a tractor for much of the day."

Despite that wistful note, Stuart was a happy man when we had our conversation, for earlier that morning he had completed his first successful caesarian calf birth (with considerable help from the local vet).

"I saw this heifer trying to calf. The calf wasn't big, and it was presented correctly. It was simply stuck. Anyway, after ninety minutes we had a live bull calf—and the heifer was still on her feet. Mother and son are doing fine!"

Stuart's day starts at six, when he brings in the cows. "That's a smashing job in the summer. You walk behind the cows. You see their udders full of milk, the sun is beaming down." The milking takes two hours. He checks the health of each cow—usually there will be at least one problem.

On his census form he put his working week at eighty hours. "Other dairy farmers tell me that is about average. Last week, though, I worked 100 hours—we were working on the silage system. Finishing at ten at night, eating on the job."

Stuart is married with two children. Last year the family had a week in Minorca; the year before, a week in the Algarve. There is also the odd weekend at Llandudno, and the odd day out at an agricultural show.

I explained to Stuart my theory that many English townspeople were obsessed with the notion of the country, yet were very ignorant of the reality. He said townsfolk often came asking if they could shoot on his land. He generally did not object, although he does not shoot himself. "It seems a bugger to enjoy myself maiming animals when I've spent the day looking after animals," is how he puts it. He is happy enough for vermin—foxes, pigeons, magpies, crows, rabbits—to be shot. Of an evening, however, he leaves the shooting to others and potters round his land; checking his fencing, brushing his yard, fiddling with his tractor.

He thinks that it is to some extent the fault of the farmers if townspeople are ignorant of the land. He has taken part in farm open days, with the aim of getting town children onto the land; he has also been involved in the NFU Roadshow, and taken it into the heart of Manchester.

He greatly values his privacy, the relative isolation of his life. A bridlepath passes through his farm, but only about twenty people a year use it. He says that he and other farmers find that only a very small proportion of the "outside public" cause trouble—usually by not controlling dogs, or by walking through standing corn.

He does believe, though, that some common perceptions of the countryside are simply childish. "People would have us cut back on nitrogen fertiliser, and use clover. But both the clover and the fertiliser produce nitrogen."

Then he told me with some passion: "It's the farmers who look after the countryside. We plant the hedges, we plant the trees. Farmers have made the English countryside, and they have done a good job. We've just planted 100 young trees—mainly oaks, but some beech, some chestnut, some ash. We've also planted two-thirds of a mile of hedge. We all realise that some trees will die. Or we should realise that. I'll chop a tree down if it is nearly dead. But then I'll plant another one."

I raised the vexed topic of the EC. "In the early years after we joined in 1973, there were undoubted short-term benefits. But farming expanded at a rate that was not sustainable. We produced too much, and it's harder to slow down than to accelerate. We've been trying to slow down since 1983.

"Food is the Number One industry, always will be. Nothing is more important than food. If the public see a farmer being paid not to grow food but to grow a field full of docks and nettles—they don't like it. They don't like the farmer being paid for nothing, as they see it."

Stuart's solution to this problem is to prevent the import of cheap food substitutes, and make farmers grow their own grain for feed—as he does. He believes that the English public do not realise how well fed they are. "In particular, they do not appreciate the huge choice of food that they have. Go into any supermarket and you'll see what I mean. And it's low cost, too. A pint of milk costs 30p, and a pint of beer costs well over a pound. And the gap is widening all the time."

I ask what the single biggest problem confronting English farmers is. "The disposal of waste. My father showed great foresight twenty years ago—he invested in an efficient slurry collection and storage system. The disposal is via irrigation. Many farmers are now having to spend tens of thousands on similar systems."

Stuart's final thought for me was an odd one: "Farming," he insisted, "is going to become full of geriatrics. It's difficult to start in farming if you're not bred to it. There's little fresh blood coming in. And it's almost impossible in these days of quotas, to make a modest start with, say, ten or a dozen cows. And with the long hours, and the social isolation, farmers' own children are being attracted away. In that sense, I cannot see my own way of life lasting much longer." (In 1990, the number of full-time farmers in the UK decreased by 9,000 to 176,000. The number of full-time farm workers fell by 7,000 to 124,000.)

After my conversation with Stuart, I headed south towards the Potteries. I had a pit stop at a marvellous country pub called the Bluebell at Spen Green—a beamed, low-ceilinged old building, with four tiny rooms. A fine pub, then, with a most friendly landlord; yet my chat with him was rather depressing. First he told me that his hand-pumped Greenalls Bitter was no longer made by Greenalls, but by Tetleys. The venerable old independent brewer now confined its business to selling beer, rather than making it.

I said it was pleasant to be in a pub that was just that, rather than a restaurant masquerading as a pub. He agreed (well he would, I suppose) saying that in some Cheshire pubs, when you walked in every single table was laid out for a meal with a "reserved" sign on it. If you wanted to sit, you might be allowed to sit at the bar, if you were lucky. He told me of a friend of his who had been in a big Cheshire pub one evening; he had not eaten a thing, but the next day his jersey stank of grease and chip oil.

Yet the money was in food, not beer, this publican told me. So he couldn't really blame his fellow publicans. Beer sales were not healthy, and he could not see them picking up.

Somewhat discouraged by this conversation—it was a superb pub, yet I left thinking it was an anachronism—I continued south. The juxtaposition from pastoral and gentle Cheshire to the mottled, scarred cityscape that I found in the Five Towns was sudden, almost brutal; but then England abounds in such dramatic changes of scene.

That evening I went for a long walk across the northern margins of the unlovely clutter of grim towns that now comprise the single borough of Stoke-on-Trent. The most famous son of these parts, after Sir Stanley Matthews and Josiah Wedgwood, is the novelist Arnold Bennett, who was born in Hanley in 1867. Maybe wisely, he upped and left when he was twenty-two, never to return more than fleetingly; he continued, for all that, to celebrate the townscapes of his youth in his fiction. He is the prosaic poet of the grimy English cityscape par excellence.

I started my perambulation to the north of Newcastle-under-Lyme, at Wolstanton; the church bells of St Margaret's were ringing, and children were at play on a vast green; a pleasant enough scene. I walked downhill by St Margaret's graveyard, past a small garage where frenetic work was being done on several cars, and gazed at the doleful aspect which now spread before me. Immediately beneath was the inevitable retail park, serviced by roads without pavements (parts of many English towns are becoming little more than successions of gap sites, punctuated by the odd gross megastore which can be reached only by car). Beyond that, the very busy dual carriageway of the A500; beyond that, a railway line; and beyond that, a sewage works and the huge gloomy fortress-like plant of British Steel Shelton. And beyond that, though it was well hidden by the steelworks, was the site of the 1986 Garden Festival. And finally, in the distance, terraces of dark, mean-looking houses straggled along the far ridges.

The part of Stoke immediately before me was called Etruria, a lovely name, but unfortunately it was the most godforsaken place I had come across. Or so I thought, as I scrambled down to the A500. (My intention was to examine what permanent legacy had been bequeathed to the community by the garden festival, but it was not easy to get to the site on foot; this landscape had not been designed for walkers. Mind you, it was apparently not designed for drivers either. As I walked along beside the A500 I was stopped no less than three times by drivers seeking directions. Of course, I was unable to help any of them. All three complained of the diabolical signposting in the area. The borough of Stoke, please note.)

I turned up Etruria Road, by now in a thoroughly negative

frame of mind. And then I met a lady walking her dog. She pointed out Josiah Wedgwood's roundhouse, which was almost immediately beneath me—the only remaining part of the original Etruria factory built by Wedgwood in 1769. It is tucked away beside the Trent and Mersey Canal, which slinks furtively under Etruria Road. I certainly would have missed this industrial landmark had it not been for the helpful lady, and I thanked her.

She then showed me Josiah Wedgwood's house up the hill, and indicated where a large hotel was being built alongside it. She told me there was a lovely lake beyond, on the garden festival site. It was "just like the country". She added: "Everything has improved so much around here since the festival." And she bade me good evening.

After this encounter my mood changed. There was something so decent, so strong and straightforward, in this woman's love of her neighbourhood that I felt small for sneering at it, as I had been doing minutes earlier. I walked round Hanley, the biggest of the Five Towns. It was dominated by a colossal shopping centre, unimaginatively called the Potteries. But, uplifted by the lady's enthusiasm for her environs, I determined to sneer no more.

Eventually I returned along Etruria Road, crossed the A500, and climbed up to Hilltop Avenue, high above the vista I had disparaged earlier. Beside the avenue was a series of allotments, where intense men were digging stolidly, tending their patches with consummate concentration, apparently unaware of the vast industrial backdrop behind them. Beside these allotments, on a patch of waste scrub, a large tent had been erected. Children were playing beside it. A thin, gaunt Lowryesque man was walking his dog across the scrub. I continued on my way back towards Wolstanton, past a little street called Bleak Street, listening for the sound of St Margaret's bells, pondering on the strangeness of England, its dignity and its pride.

CHAPTER TWELVE

DOWNHILL ALL THE WAY

Wigan—Preston

Outside the TU Unemployment Centre, Newmarket St, Wigan, an assorted group of people, most of them wearing red T-shirts, are limbering up. Sleeping bags and rucksacks are being loaded into three minibuses, one of which has loudspeakers on its roof. A man with close-cropped hair, brandishing a megaphone, is yelling instructions.

Day Two of the People's March for Jobs, 1991, is about to start. There are fifty walkers, and they come in all shapes and sizes. There are three women; the rest are men. A few are young, most are middle-aged.

I spot Tommy McIntyre, who now has his long hair in a pony tail. I tell him he is looking in good shape; he says he does not feel it. The first day, from Manchester (14.4 per cent unemployment) to Wigan (8.2 per cent) via Bolton (8.3 per cent) had tired him out. They had walked twenty-seven miles, but what had "knackered" him were the two longish stops they had had to make because of traffic congestion. "I sat in one of the vans each time, and that was a big mistake. I got stiff and sore and it was terrible when we started again."

Dear Country

I am introduced to Terry Abbott and Terry Egan, the march organisers. Terry Egan is the man with the megaphone. He has a cruel sense of humour. He tells me we have to set off at 6 m.p.h., keep going at that pace, and play a football match at Skelmersdale. Terry Abbott, a dapper, moustached figure, has the easy job; he drives the lead minibus. He tells me that the marchers are unemployed workers from each of the TU centres through the North-west, plus a few who have newly been made redundant, like Stuart Hart, an ex-Copperknob worker from Skelmersdale.

We are sent off with a speech from Roger Stott, the local Labour MP. He speaks for some minutes but his remarks may be summed up thus: it is necessary to elect a Labour Government. I sense that he is preaching to the converted. Then, at last, we are on our way. Just one banner is held aloft at the front. The rear minibus blasts out the theme from *Chariots of Fire*, and then Pavarotti singing *Nessun Dorma*, and then—eccentric choice—Ray Davies and the Kinks singing *Lola*, a hit from 1970.

Terry Abbott leads us on what seems an interminable route round the centre of Wigan. The people are hardly crowding the pavements to cheer us on our way, but for the most part there is a friendly response from those passers-by who do stop and stare. Terry Egan, with his megaphone, makes sure that everyone knows what the march is all about. Some motorists give the thumbs-up sign, a few toot their horns and grin. I notice that the workers we pass—builders, painters, postmen, van drivers—look somewhat embarrassed, and for the most part try to ignore us.

I soon realise that, despite the slow speed at which he is driving, Terry Abbott is quite ruthless in his trailblazing. He ignores red lights, and lets nothing stop him rolling along at a steady 3 m.p.h. Where necessary, Terry Egan runs forward to hold up opposing traffic. (Terry Abbott tells me later that he is determined on this second day not to repeat the mistakes of the first, when the marchers were held up by traffic and suffered consequent stiffness and soreness. Although the traffic is at times quite seriously delayed—we soon have a long queue of cars, buses and lorries behind us—the other road users seem patient; there is no anger or aggression.)

There is some banter, but the mood of the marchers is basically serious. There is determined intensity about them. What talk there is centres on trade union affairs; there is some bitter comment to the effect that the fewer members unions have, the more officials they seem to require. There is also resentment at the way in which the unions for the most part ignore the unemployed.

Then, as we get into a rhythm, talking is kept to a minimum. I notice there is a great variety of footwear on display, some of it not too suitable. Trainers are favoured by most of the marchers; Sean Keeley is sporting a stylish pair of desert boots. The musical accompaniment continues to change. To my surprise, there is no Billy Bragg. Eventually there is some Bob Marley reggae, which seems more popular than any of the other offerings.

We pass an exceedingly rundown-looking taxi office. An old bald man at the window points in agitation to a handprinted sign: DRIVERS WANTED. He gesticulates at us and keeps pointing to the sign. This is greeted with some derision.

After we have crossed over the M6, the context changes. We are now in a more genteel landscape. We are entering the upmarket area of Up Holland ("Up Yours", shouts one of the marchers as we pass the sign) and we are walking past detached houses with burglar alarms. There is now nobody to be seen on the pavements.

Terry, the martinet with the megaphone, exhorts us to greater effort. "Big hill coming up lads," he yells. "We'll have broken the back of it in three miles." He shouts at motorists held up on the other side of the road: "If you hate Norman Lamont, toot your horns." (Norman Lamont had recently suggested that unemployment was an acceptable political price to pay for the conquest of inflation.) Terry shouts this several times, but no-one toots. Either no-one in Up Holland knows who Norman Lamont is, or he is remarkably popular. I mentioned this to Terry: he changes "Norman Lamont" to "The Chancellor". Now one or two people toot.

Halfway up the long hill, the road widens. We pull into the side to let the long tailback of traffic past. Terry yells at the cars: "You have been held up by the People's March for Jobs—remember to tell your grandchildren . . . if these people had jobs, you wouldn't have been held up . . . Write to John Major and complain to him about this unseemly rabble who have held you up." But there is still no unpleasantness or aggression; not, that is, until we come to the fringes of Skelmersdale (unemployment 12.9 per cent).

Terry Abbott moves the lead minibus on to a large roundabout and Terry Egan holds up his hand to halt oncoming cars. But the first car, a red Fiesta, is driven by an angry-looking man (who has the aspect of a worker rather than a boss). He toots, gesticulates, and swerves right through the marchers. "Maybe he's got to get to his job," says one of them, wryly. Another mutters: "Come the revolution, we'll have to waste some bastards." This is the only bitter moment.

We are walking downhill now. One of the older marchers says: "We've been going downhill for years."

We are given a warm welcome, and lunch, at the Quarrybank Community Club, just outside Skelmersdale. Over a beer, Terry Abbott tells me about the march strategy. It was to mark the tenth anniversary of the 1981 March for Jobs, which had generated much publicity—and also led to the nationwide network of TU Unemployment Centres. The 1981 march had converged on London, but Terry admitted that there did not appear to be the nationwide will—or money—to mount a repeat exercise. So the north-west TUC had organised a local march, not just to commemorate the first one, but also to focus attention on unemployment levels in the region. These were particularly bad (19 per cent) in Liverpool, where the march was to end.

Terry, a thoughtful man, felt there were dangers in the "discovery" of unemployment in the south-east. People there had been hard hit by the 1991 recession, while most of them had sailed through the one ten years earlier. He thought that political and media attention might focus so much on the south-east, where the problems of unemployment had some novelty—and shock—value, that regions like the north-west would be ignored. And the danger for local people was that they could become inured to unemployment, conditioned to it, as if it were an everyday fact of life, something to be lived with and tolerated. It was essential for people to keep fighting and protesting. It was essential to prevent all discussion of unemployment focussing on the south-east.

Terry Abbott did not say so, but I thought I detected an undercurrent in all this: a subtext of resentment. The Conservatives won the 1983 and 1987 elections despite very high national rates of unemployment, which as an issue was nonetheless not at the top of the national political agenda. But when unemployment suddenly scarred the south-east, it shot to the top of that agenda. Indeed, it became the burning political issue of the moment. It was almost as if England could tolerate—or comfortably forget—unemployment in the north. But let it hit the south, and the media and politicians would take notice. Here was another refinement of the north-south divide.

Some of the people I marched with had been unemployed for ten years and more. For ten years, Terry said, they had been forgotten. By all means, he said, get indignant about the new unemployed in the south. But don't, in doing so, forget the others.

I raised one other point with Terry: Why was there not a police escort? He said that the authorities had been given full details of the march, and that the police had approved the route. They had had a police motorcycle escort out of Manchester, but after that they had been left on their own. He suspected this was because the police were seriously undermanned and their resources were stretched to the limit.

I took my leave of the marchers, as I had to get back to Wigan. I was given directions to Skelmersdale town centre by a woman in the club, but I soon got lost. Skelmersdale was clearly not designed for pedestrians; it seemed to consist of broad roads and vast roundabouts, and nothing else. Certainly no pavements. I asked a man filling his ancient Volvo at a petrol station. He pointed me in the correct direction. Two minutes later, I heard a toot as I walked along the grass beside the road. It was the man in the Volvo, offering me a lift. "Magic roundabouts, that's Skem, magic roundabouts," he said delphically. "Alternatively, we call this the Skelmersdale triangle. Once in, you never get out. Some people drive round for hours before they realise they're lost. Terrible place, Skelmersdale."

He dropped me off at the huge shopping concourse which was being further expanded. It was incredibly busy. There was a long line of black taxis, but they were being gobbled up at a great rate. I asked the first available driver to take me back to Wigan. He turned out to be a Scot. "Terrible place, this," he said, as we pulled out.

Back in Wigan, before moving on to Preston, I had a quick look at Wigan Pier, made world-famous by George Orwell, who could not find it. It has been turned, predictably, into a tourist attraction. There was a big pub, inevitably called the Orwell—and, on the other side of the canal, a "nightspot". A permanent historical exhibition called *The Way We Were* features actors and actresses playing various roles from the past. Water-buses ply up and down the canal. I suppose it could be worse.

As I left Wigan, one of the recurring north-south rows, so much a feature of the English sociological repertoire, was brewing, if that is the right word. England's biggest off-licence chain had decided to call some of its shops—in places like Wigan—by the simple designation of DRINKS STORES. In supposedly better class areas they were to be called WINE SHOPS and, in the very poshest areas, they were to be called WINE RACKS. A spokesman for the chain had pontificated thus: "You are going to intimidate people if you display Château Lafite when they want Newcastle Brown. It is unreasonable to expect the same tastes in Wimbledon as in Wigan."

The aforementioned Roger Stott MP had blasted right back: "To offer a better service to some people is preposterous, and could only have been dreamed up by a southerner who hasn't a clue about our quality of life. This firm has categorised us as lower class, and therefore unable to appreciate good service and decent wine.

"It begs the question: What are the downmarket people of Wigan going to get in their downmarket DRINK STORES? Sawdust on the floors and spittoons in the corner?"

A routine row, if you want, but one that says much about England today.

And so on to Preston, a town with a rich past and a poor present. Cobbett stood for Parliament here; so did Henry "Orator" Hunt, the greatest demagogue England has ever known. Hunt was successful, Cobbett wasn't. As the industrial revolution rolled on, Preston workers stood up for their rights; they gained a reputation for radicalism and militancy unequalled elsewhere in Lancashire. Preston employers matched them: they were reckoned to be the toughest and most brutal in the county.

Dickens visited Preston—"a nasty place", he called it—during a protracted strike which involved as many as 30,000 of the town's workers. His attitude to industrial action was ambivalent, to say the least. Nonetheless his visit inspired *Hard Times*, the most direct fictive assault on the degradation and alienation brought about by swift and insensitive industrialisation. It is, by his standards, an unusually short and tightly disciplined novel.

Coketown, the drab town which is its setting, is Preston.

> It was a town of machinery and tall chimneys, out of which interminable serpents of smoke trailed themselves for ever and ever, and never got uncoiled. It had a black canal in it, and a river that ran purple with ill-smelling dye, and vast piles of buildings full of windows where there was a rattling and a trembling all day long, and where the piston of the steam-engine worked monotonously up and down, like the head of an elephant in a state of melancholy madness. It contained several large streets all very like one another, and many small streets still more like one

another, inhabited by people equally like one another, who all went in and out at the same hours, with the same sound upon the same pavements, to do the same work, and to whom every day was the same as yesterday and tomorrow, and every year the counterpart of the last and the next.

Although industrial employers are keenly satirised in the novel, the most vicious satire is reserved not for an employer but for Slackbridge, the slimy and unctuous union agitator. Slackbridge has a relatively small role, but it is nonetheless significant that Dickens made a workers' leader by far the most repellent of his characters.

In the nineteenth century, as today, Preston had a multiplicity of pubs. In 1830 the population was about 50,000 (and growing rapidly) and there were already 200 pubs in the town. A decade later, the Rev. J. Clay wrote: "The mortality of the town chiefly predominates among the children of the working classes, the mortality among them increasing as the social condition of the parent sinks . . . additional causes are connected with the ignorance, indifference, neglect or selfishness of the parents. Their ignorance leads them to give their offspring the most improper food even when they are able to procure for them wholesome sustenance; and too often the child is destroyed by the gin poured into it with the intention to nourish it." (There are echoes here of another cleric, The Rev. Ian Johnson, talking about his Lancashire parish 150 years on.)

Preston children were given, according to Clay, beer and spirits to keep them quiet. He reported that more than 1600 families used Godfrey's Cordial, a compound containing opium.

Preston's collective drink problem engendered various responses. The most notable was perhaps the birth of the Teetotal movement; the town became known as the "Jerusalem of Teetotalism". At a public meeting in 1833, a reformed drunk called Dicky Turner told the assembled throng that so-called moderate drinking was not the answer to their problems: "I'll have nowt to do wi' this moderation, botheration pledge: I'll be reet down and out tee-tee-total for ever and ever," he announced.

Thus, according to the local historian Frank Graham, teetotalism was born. The Preston Temperance Advocate was launched, and published monthly.

It had little effect.

Nowadays Preston is a sorry town, a mixture of grim terraces, drab high-rise blocks and pocked gap sites. It has one characterful street, the Friargate, in which higgledy-piggledy two-storey buildings lean crazily into each other; this street at least has some interesting shops, and some fine pubs.

Just beyond one end of Friargate are the main buildings of Lancashire Polytechnic. I visited the Racial Equality Unit there to meet Yasmin Ali, who has established a reputation as one of the north-west's most thoughtful commentators on racial tensions.

Preston was the first place in England to have a demonstration against Salman Rushdie's novel *The Satanic Verses*. A small group broke away from the main demonstration and raided a local bookstore, where they knocked over bookstands; another splinter group invaded another bookshop and a knife was allegedly pulled on the manager. Before the book became a national issue, it had been completely withdrawn from sale in Preston.

Talking to Yasmin Ali and her colleagues in the unit, I formed the impression that Preston was an inward-looking community, socially and politically. The local ethnic communities reflected this introversion, suggesting that in one respect anyway they had been well integrated, certainly better integrated than similar communities in the south of England. A local survey recently indicated that Muslims did not care what happened in their children's primary schools as long as they were learning to read and write; in other words, Muslim concerns were basically no different from white concerns.

Local race relations, I was told, had been greatly exacerbated by the Gulf War. Muslim workers were sent home from the nearby Royal Ordnance factory during the course of the war, which had generated much anti-Arab feeling. It was a small step from that to more generalised anti-Muslim feeling. There was some British Movement activity on local estates, and a Ku-Klux Klan leaflet had been distributed.

"In some ways it feels worse here than in Manchester," Yasmin Ali told me. "In Manchester there is more organised racism—so more organised anti-racism. Where you have organised movements, you end up with almost ritualised warfare between defined groups, but that in a way makes it safer. Here it is hard, if not impossible, to identify the people who are responsible for racial attacks."

She told me she had been terrified four years earlier after a particularly gruesome local murder, an arson attack. Three students—two Asians and a white—had died. It turned out that race was not a factor in the attack. But for some time Yasmin Ali was desperately scared—and so, she said, were many of her colleagues.

Yasmin Ali was born in England; her people come from Bangladesh. "I grew up in Birmingham, on a predominantly white council estate. We experienced a lot of verbal harassment. Up here my experience has been different. The prejudice is more subtle. In the polytechnic, I have suffered from academic, middle-class prejudice. For example, there are six members of this unit. Only one of us is white. People come and ask for him (her white colleague). If he's not here, they immediately turn and go away. None of the rest of us will do. We are not white."

I asked if she regarded herself as English. "Yes, definitely. I became aware of how English the communities I work with here are when I compare them with, say, the Turks in Germany. They are not German at all.

"I think the problem of Englishness is the problem of Britishness. It is straightforward for Welshmen, or Scots, to feel at ease with their identity. English people have more difficulty in identifying with England simply because of the ease with which people use the terms as if they are interchangeable. But I certainly feel more English than Bangladeshi."

What was a useful symbol of England, a focus of Englishness?

"The language, I suppose. I even dream in English."

We talked a little about the north–south tensions in England, tensions which people in the north seem much more aware of, and concerned about. "In southern England, Preston is perceived as being very, very unglamorous. It's refreshing to go to Holland or Germany, where the place you come from is not perceived as being unglamorous—just English."

She conceded that there was at times an excessive northern chauvinism. But she added: "Even as a Midlander, I have always resented London's derision. Now we can have a better relationship with Europe than with London. And it's actually easier to get to Amsterdam from here than it is to get to London."

Then, through the good offices of the unit, I met a young, very petite black girl, who had been attacked by a skinhead. Various people had told me that racism in England was becoming more discreet, less overt; and even if this was insidious, it was surely preferable to violence. But violence still takes place, all too often. The girl said she would tell me about the incident on the understanding that I would not identify her.

It was not, as physical attacks go, particularly severe, although of course all such attacks are serious. What was of special interest, indeed what worried me most, was the reaction of this highly intelligent girl of twenty-four to the attack. But first, here, in her own words, is what happened:

"It was about ten to eight in the morning. I was conscious that I was going to be early for work for once, and was feeling quite pleased with myself. Then I saw a bloke in front of me. He was not involved in the attack, but he distracted me. I had to step aside. Then this skinhead lunged at me. He seemed to come from nowhere—actually it was a car lot. He started kicking me, really hard. As he kicked me, he was shouting things. I couldn't hear what they were, but I knew it was a racial attack.

"I managed, instinctively, to run onto the road. Cars had to swerve to avoid hitting me. The skinhead—he was huge—ran off. I stayed on the road and the cars just drove round me. Not one car stopped. Nobody helped me."

She was badly hurt, both physically and mentally. I asked if she had gone to the police. She laughed with derision. I could not understand this derision, and I pressed her.

"There would be *no point*," she said. "The police don't know anything. They don't understand. This kind of thing is just part of life in England for people like me. The police refuse to take any interest. They would not have paid any attention. I would have been politely ignored. I know that."

In fact she did not tell anybody about the attack for some time. Then she confided in a black colleague, and then a white one.

"I expect physical attacks to happen," she said, in a matter-of-fact way. Then she added an extraordinary thought: "In a way, it is the more subtle discrimination that frightens me more. People in England have become quite sophisticated bigots, you know. I'm obviously not talking about the likes of the skinhead now. I'm talking about managers, people with power. They have been trained and taught not to discriminate, so they just discriminate more subtly."

Like Yasmin Ali, this girl came from the Midlands. She gave Preston a pretty grim report. "I don't like the town. And I don't like the hills around it. They're somehow threatening. And it's permanently wet here. And the town empties in the evenings—except for young men who go to the pubs to get drunk. I don't really like this part of England at all." And who could blame her?

From Preston I moved on eastwards to Blackburn, where I joined the M65, yet another of England's eccentric motorways. This one swings north-west for a few miles, and then peters out at the steep mill town of Colne, where I met Mr Leslie Illingworth, who is general secretary of England's second smallest trade union, the Society of Shuttlemakers.

Mr Illingworth is a proud man, proud of his craft and proud of his union. In 1950 there were almost 600 shuttlemakers in the society, representing about 90 per cent of English shuttle-makers. But with the coming of shuttleless looms, and the closure of mills all over the north of England, the membership dwindled drastically. Now there are only twenty members, six of whom are honorary or retired.

Despite this the society maintains three branches, an executive committee which meets four times a year at the Cornholme home of the president, Mr Clarence Brown, and an annual general meeting. The most recent AGM, marking the centenary of the society's founding, was held in Todmorden Town Hall in March 1991. Four members attended.

The main excitement at the meeting—the only excitement, if truth be told—concerned the venue for the society's anniversary outing. Nelson Branch had suggested the Isle of Man, to coincide with the TT races (I suspect there the influence of Mr Illingworth, who has a motorbike and used to be a speedway rider) but Todmorden Branch came up with a counter proposal: a trip to London. "But they were too late," Mr Illingworth told me with a grin and just a hint of retrospective triumph. "Todmorden had not got their proposal minuted from the previous meeting, so it was not competent business."

And so the Isle of Man it was, and a good time was had by all, or at least by the twelve members who attended. "We had £25,000 in the kitty before the outing—now it's down to £23,000," said Mr Illingworth with another grin.

I asked if other, bigger, unions had ever tried to take over the society. "Oh yes," said Mr Illingworth. "We've had approaches from two unions, including the TGWU. But none of us wants to be swallowed up. The funds have been built up and I don't want another union to get our money. The big unions have their bosses with big offices and big cars. I don't see why our money should go to people who know nothing about shuttlemaking."

What would happen if the society folded? "We're realistic, and I have thought about that. If the union—or the three shops that still make shuttles in England – fold up, then we'd simply divide the money among the members. The members would certainly not benefit at all if we were taken over by a big union, you can be sure of that. And, as I say, these big unions are run by people who know nothing about shuttlemaking."

Not many people in England know much about shuttlemaking these days. As Mr Illingworth said, there are only three shuttlemaking factories left; and almost all the shuttles produced by them go to the Far East. At Mr Illingworth's firm, Halsteads of Nelson, there are five shuttlemakers and two apprentices.

"My apprenticeship took six years but it's just three years now. The apprentices get just £60 a week. When I started it was a well-paid job. Now you can get more for labouring."

Mr Illingworth then showed me his collection of over thirty shuttles, the finest being made of persimmon and hornbeam, the inferior ones of boxwood. The shuttle is a symbol of England's industrial past; the decline of the Society reflects the passing of an era.

"It was given two years, no more, when I joined it twenty-eight years ago. As I say, we have discussed what would happen if it folded. But I'd like to see it last another twenty-eight years. That's the extent of my ambition. They said it was dead when I joined. It's not dead yet.

"There are no politics, though. We've never been on strike. What's the point? We know our bosses on a personal basis. We negotiate with them directly. The relations at my shop, Halsteads, are very good."

Leslie Illingworth has a son, Joseph, who is four. I asked if he could envisage Joseph as a shuttlemaker. "No," he said sadly. "I'm afraid I can't. I can't see any long-term future in it at all."

The society's fees are £1 a week (50p for apprentices). The union remains a paid-up member of the TUC, though it does not send a delegation to the annual congress. "It would cost too much," said Mr Illingworth. "It would mean time off work, and travel expense. And we'd probably not have as good a time as we had on our outing.

"I mean," he added philosophically, "we'd just be a small fish in a big pond, wouldn't we?"

A NOTE ON TRANSPORT

This book describes a journey of 5,000 miles round England. I drove these miles in my car, using public transport very rarely—the tube in London a few times, a train from Preston to Manchester and back, a bus along the coast of West Sussex. I regret this; I would have preferred to use public transport for two reasons. First, if you are travelling with other people, particularly local people, you are more likely to get the feel of the area you are passing through than if you are insulated and alone in a private car. Secondly, I genuinely like trains. I normally travel at least 20,000 miles a year by train—and I would love to have undertaken this journey by train, where feasible. But since the Beeching cuts of the 1960s, many parts of England—and not all of them obscure parts—are simply not served by trains. To have travelled by a mixture of bus and train might have been possible, had I had much more time at my disposal. But, as Andy Medhurst of Sussex University remarked to me, it would have taken about three years to travel round England by public transport.

In the event, travelling by car did give me some insights into the English character. I saw hardly any instances of rude or aggressive driving. The English are courteous, efficient and patient drivers. They also strike me as being proud of their cars, which on the whole they keep clean and smart. The contrast with—say—the French, who drive with little consideration for others and have a very insouciant attitude to bumps, scrapes and dirt on their cars, could not be more marked.

Indeed, the pride of the English in their cars, and the care and concern with which they drive, are brought out in the comparative road death and injury statistics. Driving in England is much safer than driving on the Continent. There are 9.7 road deaths per 100,000 people in Britain (the lowest rate in Europe) compared with 12 per 100,000 in Italy, 13 in Germany and 20 in France. These statistics refer to Britain, not England, but they reflect well on England for English roads are much more overcrowded than Scottish or Welsh roads. Indeed, English roads are the most overcrowded in Europe. Yet despite that there were fewer road deaths in England in 1990-91 than there were in any year since 1948. As Malcolm Rifkind, the current Minister of Transport, says: "We are the safest country in the world so far as road safety is concerned. The vast majority of our motorists are sensible and safe drivers." That may reek of complacency, but I think the evidence, both subjective and objective, endorses his upbeat view.

Again, the very privacy of the car no doubt appeals to the English, this most private of peoples. (George Orwell thought that the privateness of English life was one of its principal characteristics.) That may well be a reason why the English, despite constant efforts to persuade them to use an admittedly underfunded and overstretched public transport system, continue to resist those efforts defiantly.

But if the English like, even love, their cars, they cannot love their roads. Too many of them are grotesquely congested. There are not enough motorways. London, for some reason, is nothing like so well served by motorways as Greater Manchester, which has 250 miles of motorway in its immediate environs. Altogether, England has only 1,500 miles of motorway. Yet this is the nation which has more cars per roadmile than any other country in Europe; and the nation which has allowed its railway network to be so run down that (forgetting just for the moment about passengers) trains now carry only 6 per cent of its freight, compared with 45 per cent forty years ago. This is the country which has almost 25 million cars, vans, lorries and juggernauts crowding on to just 200,000 miles of road.

Despite the almost farcical paucity of motorways, some of the existing ones—the M180, for example—seem underused and superfluous. Meanwhile, other routes are crying out for motorways: there is a huge need for an east-west motorway across the south of England, to take one instance. The M27, which bypasses Southampton and Portsmouth, should surely be extended eastwards all the way to Dover. The worst persistent congestion I encountered—and I encountered plenty—was on the A27 in Sussex.

Yet even to whisper that new motorways should be built, or that an existing one should be extended, is to invite anger and perhaps fury from rural conservationists, the people who can readily, and if need be angrily, invoke the traditional arcadian—and agrarian—values of England, the people whom the Rt Hon. Dr John Gilbert scathingly describes as Umclouts—Upper Middle Class Louts.

When I stopped briefly in the town of Ilkley in Yorkshire, I became aware of a bitter controversy about a new by-pass which was being proposed for the town. The controversy seemed to focus not so much on whether the by-pass was needed—it clearly was—as on whether it would be the first phase of a great new transPennine motorway, an extension of the M65 which currently goes at a north-west angle from Blackburn to Colne, a great new motorway that would curve round from Colne via Skipton and Ilkley to Leeds, thus supplementing the already overburdened M62. This conjecture was already raising passions in the area. Motorways and potential motorways raise virulent feeling in rural England; the recent building of a motorway through the country to the north of Oxford was not achieved without much dissent, bitterness and even heartbreak.

Some transport strategists also contend that the building of new motorways is in itself no solution, for the motorways only create a new demand; they thus create congestion rather than relieve it. There is obviously some point to this argument, though I suspect it only obtains in certain contexts (most notably the M25 orbital motorway round London).

The roads lobby in England consistently points out that while almost £20 billion a year is collected in tax from motorists and the road freight industry, only about 20 per cent of that sum is actually invested in the transport infrastructure. Current spending on road maintenance is only about £500 million a year (£300 million of that is spent on motorways and trunk routes). This is at least an improvement on the performance under the last Labour Government, when there was for a time a moratorium on road building and refurbishment.

Despite the comparatively miserly sum being spent on the repair and maintenance of England's roads, I seemed to come across a constant succession of roadworks. I like to be punctual and I was determined not to turn up late for any appointments. Despite grappling with some obscure one-way systems, and some strange towns and villages that were poorly signposted, I soon found that the only significant impediment to efficient journey planning consisted of the seemingly ubiquitous roadworks.

I came to dread the triangular roadworks sign and its intimation of the inevitable delays and tailbacks ahead. And it occurred to me when I passed yet another triumphant contractor's sign boasting of an improvement scheme being completed months ahead of schedule—I remember in particular one at the Pevensey by-pass in Sussex, proclaiming that the work had been completed nine months in advance of the target date—that England's roads are being constructed, or reconstructed, too swiftly and too skimpily. Perhaps if a little more attention were paid to deeper foundations and more durable surfaces, English road users would suffer fewer roadworks; they would not have to run so hard to stand still.

When I was travelling round England, one of the bestsellers was a book by the comedian Ben Elton called *Gridlock*. I suspect that "gridlock" is going to become one of the most overused words in the England of the 1990s. The phenomenon of the superjam has already hit London; early in 1991 a fire just off Bishopsgate in the City led within an hour or so to a fifty-square-mile gridlock. As the firefighters sealed off streets in the vicinity of Shoreditch and Bishopsgate, the centre of London became, inexorably, one colossal traffic jam. An academic later calculated that the jam had spread outwards in all directions at the speed of four miles per hour. The fire had started at the worst possible time, just as the morning rush-hour traffic was starting to build up. Even so, its effects were soon felt as far away as the M40, beyond London's West End.

Of course, it could well be that fewer commuters would use their cars if a superior rail and tube service were provided, despite what I wrote above about public transport. But the service provided by Network South-east in the commuter routes round London is so woefully inadequate that passenger numbers actually decreased by seven per cent in the first half of 1991. The rolling stock is often at least thirty years old; and it is not only clapped out, it is also filthy and, generally, vandalised. Two years ago when I travelled into Fenchurch St on a grievously overcrowded early morning commuter train from Southend with the MP for Southend East, Sir Teddy Taylor, he told me that he had often seen, at night, passengers quietly and systematically vandalising the trains. They offered no threat to their fellow passengers; they just proceeded to break up the trains with quiet intensity.

The tube, which has suffered from overuse and underinvestment, is if anything, even worse. Elsewhere I note that the chairman of London Underground, no less, described his own network as "an appalling shambles, an infrastructure that had been neglected for thirty years".

To add insult to injury, public transport in London is not cheap. Indeed it is just about the most expensive in Europe. A recent survey of Europe's ten leading cities by the Association of London Authorities indicated that public transport in London was, by a considerable margin, the dearest. (Next dearest, but a long way behind, was Copenhagen. The cheapest cities were Athens, Paris, Rome and Madrid.)

In view of all this, it is surprising that transport has not been higher up the English political agenda. But the Department of Transport has traditionally been regarded by high-flying ministers as a Cinderella portfolio and there has been a rapid turnover of transport ministers. Not one of them has made any kind of national impact in the job since the days of the Tory Ernie Marples, in the early 1960s—and then Labour's Barbara Castle later in the 1960s.

When the Rt Hon. Dr John Gilbert, whose views are quoted at some length elsewhere in this book, was Transport Minister in a Labour Government, he was not even in the Cabinet. When Mrs Thatcher came to power in 1979, she kept her first Transport Minister, Norman Fowler, out of the Cabinet. He was eventually elevated into the Cabinet, but soon changed jobs; thereafter Mrs Thatcher, who had little interest in transport policy and a thorough dislike of the railways, changed her transport ministers with regularity; not one of them even began to impose himself on the job.

The current incumbent, Malcolm Rifkind, has been producing plenty of mouth music about a switch in priorities, a switch back to the railways. And when I spoke to the railmen of Crewe, they seemed confident that chronic congestion on the roads was willy-nilly going to swing people back to the railways, whatever the politicians did or did not do.

Yet, I wonder. I suspect, as I suggested earlier, that the English, in a quiet, proud way, actually love their cars—they love the independence, the freedom and, above all, the privacy that their vehicles afford them. As for trains, I reckon that English trains will tend in time to become supertrains like the French TGV, high-speed machines for whisking businessmen and other fatcats from city to city at enormous speed.

It is not a customary insight, and no doubt it is not a welcome one, but I sense that the English, who gave trains to the world, are now turning their collective back on this, still potentially the most romantic of all forms of transport, and have instead embraced the motor car, derided and despised as it is.

Meanwhile I ought to confess, as a Scot, that in Scotland we have no real understanding of the transport problems so many English people face daily. Two recent quotes from prominent politicians, one Scottish and one English, perhaps illustrate this point. First, the Scot: Malcolm Rifkind, the Transport Minister, whom I have already mentioned. He represents an Edinburgh constituency and he recently opined: "What we call traffic jams in Edinburgh are what we have in London at one o'clock in the morning." Secondly, Dr David Owen MP. On a recent visit to Glasgow Dr Owen simply declared himself

A Note on Transport

"green with envy" at the excellence of the Scottish transport infrastructure compared with that of England.

Finally, 1990 was the first year in which in the UK, sales of new bicycles outstripped sales of new cars. The number of bikes sold was 2.25 million and as I write this the indications are that that figure will be overtaken in 1991. After my experiences, recounted elsewhere, of hiring bikes in Cambridge and Brighton, I went out and bought a bike when I returned home—something I would not have dreamed of doing two years ago.

The most spectacular trend towards bike ownership and bike use appears to be in central London, where between 1988 and 1990 bicycle use increased by 40 per cent. At least half a million people are now estimated to use bikes in London at least once a week. Maybe I was partly mistaken when I suggested above that the English are in love with their cars; maybe they are rather more in love with their bikes.

Dear Country

PLAUDITS

Tourism is now desperately important to England. Travelling round the country, I stayed at a variety of hotels, drank in many pubs, ate many meals. Here is a brief list of the establishments that impressed me most, followed by a frivolous catalogue of other superlatives:

Best hotel: without a doubt, Chedington Court Hotel, at Chedington, North Dorset. Everything a country house hotel should be, but so often isn't. Chedington Court would have been run close by Chilvester Hill House at Calne—had that establishment allowed itself the status of a hotel.

Best meal: traditional English dinner cooked by Gill Dilley at Chilvester Hill House, Calne.

Best Pub: a most difficult choice. I found two almost perfect country pubs in Lancashire (a very fecund county for pubs, incidentally)—the Martin Inn near Burscough and the Myerscough on the A59 near Balderstone, where the welcome was particularly friendly—but both of them placed a heavy, possibly over heavy, emphasis on the serving of meals, and I tend to agree with the traditionalists: pubs are for drinking, not eating.

The most pleasant pub I encountered was the Bluebell at Spen Green (near Astbury), a real gem tucked away in the pastoral hinterland of South Cheshire. The landlord was most affable, if lugubrious about the future of the licensed trade.

Best motorway service area: did not exist. But the worst (and there was lot of competition here) was Charnock Richard, on the M6 just south of Preston.

Best beer: I greatly enjoyed my morning at Bateman's Brewery, Salem Bridge, Wainfleet, and so sentiment suggests that Bateman's XXXB Bitter should be the choice. But I have yet to drink a finer English beer than Greene King's celestial Abbot Ale.

Best cheese: Sage Derby.

Best village name: a draw between Claxby Pluckacre, Lincolnshire and Ryme Intrinseca, Dorset.

Best pub name: a draw between The Generous Briton, Brant Broughton and The Vulture's Perch, Kentish Town, Camden.

Best county: Lincolnshire—vast, varied, forgotten, almost forlorn, waiting to be discovered and celebrated.

Best building: Lincoln Cathedral.

Best parish church: St Oswald's, Ashbourne.

Town with most potential: Dover.

Most unprepossessing town: Preston.

Most dynamic place: Manchester.

Dirtiest place: Manchester.

Friendliest people: Mancunians.

Most garrulous people: Mancunians.

Most snobbish place: Hove.

Biggest bore: inevitably, Gazza.

Best viewpoint: above Parbold, looking due west over the fertile plain of West Lancashire—partly because it was so unexpected.

Loveliest park: Kensington Gardens.

Most pitiful symbol of England: the Major Oak at Edwinstowe.

Most quintessentially English experience: open-air performance of Shakespeare's *Romeo and Juliet* by Reaction Theatre Company on a cold May evening in the Queen's Park, Brighton.

And finally—

Marginally pretentious award for the place that best suggested the quiddity of England: a draw between Bag Enderby, Lincolnshire, and Little Gidding, Cambridgeshire.

Dear Country

SUMMING UP

The previous pages describe England as I found it in the early summer of 1991. But I'd like to begin this summing up at a bleaker time, November of the previous year, and indeed at a bleak place, just about the bleakest I have found in England. I was at the Tan Hill Inn, England's highest pub, just after I'd been asked to write the book. In this somewhat forsaken context, I began seriously to ruminate on England. The inn stands high (1,732 feet above sea level, to be precise) on Arkengarthdale Moor in north-west Yorkshire. It is an isolated situation, but the Pennine Way goes more or less past its front door, and on this particular morning walkers constantly struggled past. Only a few stopped for a pint, but the inn was busy nonetheless; most of the custom had come on wheels. As I have noted elsewhere, the English love their cars. There were seventeen cars parked around the inn.

Inside, all was bustle. Despite a notice warning that the inn cat had recently attacked a dog, and that dogs were thus taken inside at their owners' risk, there were three dogs in the pub. There were also several children and a baby, and many adults. The telly was on, loudly. The man of the moment, Gazza—who else—had just launched a video, and this was being forcefully promoted on whatever programme it was that the landlord had chosen. The telly almost drowned out the conversation, but from what I could hear, that too centred on the wayward Geordie. The superstar seemed ubiquitous.

Outside there was less noise, but much activity, despite the elemental grim starkness of the moor. An extension to the pub was being built, and by the builders' clutter two tents were being struck. Walkers were scattered across the moor, following, more or less, the route of the Way. (It is dangerous to wander too much hereabouts, for there are old pit shafts all around.)

The moor is a near-wilderness. The land is not green and pleasant, but dark and scarred. To the north, however, there is a green and pastoral valley. But through it moved a constant snake of traffic: juggernauts and cars, cars and juggernauts. This is the A66, which cuts through the Pennines from Brough in the west to Scotch Corner in the east. Nowhere, but nowhere in England, are you very far from people, or from traffic.

A notice near the inn proclaims: Welcome to Richmondshire. I wonder: What on earth is Richmondshire? Actually, at this time, the Tan Hill Inn was technically in County Durham; but in 1991 the Boundary Commissioners made a popular, if minor, adjustment and the inn reverted to its pre-1974 status as a Yorkshire pub. Local loyalties are desperately important in England; and in the north of England especially, your county can be more important than your country.

The day before I was at the Tan Hill Inn, Sir Geoffrey Howe had resigned from the Government. The European debate was in full flow. I listened to a radio phone-in in which people from the north of England kept making the point that it did not matter to them if they were governed from Brussels, or Berlin for that matter—it couldn't be any worse than government from London. I was surprised by the vehemence of the anti-London feeling. Later, when I toured England, I was to hear many similar sentiments, if less strongly expressed.

Sir Geoffrey's resignation led to a cataclysmic few weeks in British politics. Mrs Thatcher eventually resigned and John Major, of whom few people had heard three years earlier, became Prime Minister. His first words to the nation were delivered in a typically low-key style, yet they implied profound dissatisfaction with his inheritance. He wanted a classless society; he wanted a country at ease with itself. John Major was talking about the UK, not just England, but—perhaps tendentiously—I sensed that his words had particular application to England.

Now Mrs Thatcher had been, without doubt, a consummate politician. She dominated British politics and her hat-trick of election victories was a remarkable achievement. Yet under her stewardship the Tory party became, essentially, an English

Dear Country

party. It has never had much influence in Northern Ireland where, like Labour, it does not put up candidates. But during Mrs Thatcher's twelve years in power, the Tories' position in Wales weakened considerably. And in Scotland their decline was even more marked. In the 1950s the Tories had dominated Scottish politics, winning more than 50 per cent of the vote in 1955. Yet by the end of the Thatcher era they were struggling desperately to hold on to even 25 per cent of the Scottish vote.

Mrs Thatcher did, however, strengthen the Tories' hold on England. She was in some respects an English nationalist; one effect of her twelve years in power was the serious weakening of the constitutional cohesion of the Union. But her political attitude to England was peculiar. This may be seen in some relief if we compare her to another Tory who had dominated British domestic politics earlier in the century, a man who was three times Prime Minister, Stanley Baldwin.

Apart from her frequent, somewhat sentimental references to her father, Alderman Roberts—she hardly ever referred to her mother—Mrs Thatcher did not invoke her Lincolnshire roots. In fact she seemed determined to distance herself from her beginnings in Grantham. She accepted London as the centre of England and no doubt the centre of the universe.

Stanley Baldwin, on the other hand, loved to get away from London. He loved to play the countryman. He constantly invoked his roots in Worcestershire, where he kept his home. Consistently, if somewhat self-consciously, Baldwin reiterated what he perceived to be the values of the English countryside. Roy Jenkins notes in his splendid biography of Baldwin that, despite this, the politician was not an English country squire: "His agricultural knowledge was very limited. He could not have milked a cow, and he poked pigs much more often in cartoons than in the farmyard. But he was a genuine West Worcestershire man . . ."

Baldwin's oratorical theme reached its climax when he made his famous speech to the Royal Society of St George. Here is the peroration: "The sounds of England, the tinkle of the hammer on the anvil in the country smithy, the corncrake on a dewy morning, the sound of the scythe against the whetstone, and the sight of the plough team coming over the brow of the hill, the sight that has been seen in England since England was a land, and may be seen in England long after the Empire has perished and every works in England has ceased to function."

If we contrast Baldwin and Thatcher we see on the one hand, the potent invocation of an eternally arcadian England, with either no, or at best slighting, references to the industrial wealth creation which powered its pre-eminence; whereas Mrs Thatcher sought to change the English political culture around the notion of enterprise. In a sense she sought to Americanise it. She certainly had no time for maudlin references to slow, unchanging rural England. She was obsessed by wealth creation.

As that most acute of commentators on how modern England is governed, Prof. Peter Hennessy, put it to me: "Mrs Thatcher was very strong politically, but very weak culturally. She really hardly understood England at all, whereas Baldwin understood it totally."

He continued: "Mrs Thatcher never understood how religion helped to push Victorian dynamism. She never understood that this process could not be repeated. Also, she never understood that money is not everything in England. The hierarchy of esteem is not money-driven. Status is not based on money. It may be in the first place: you acquire the BMW and the Armani suit, the easy symbols of wealth. But then comes the crucial second phase; green wellingtons, and a piece of the Cotswolds."

Hennessy believes that while the current reality in the English country is by no means idyllic—"look at the lager louts, the near-riots, the local rivalries, the nastiness to incomers, the bitchiness"—the political invocation of the green and pleasant land, and in particular its villages, could still strike a chord in the very recent past, and can continue to do so today.

"I think that this was particularly the case in the 1970s. The IMF might have been here, in effect running the country—but there would always be an England nonetheless. There would always be the well-ordered country life, with the most beautiful villages in the world, and their wonderful churches. This was an image, an ideal, of almost eternal significance, to be used at times of failure, and there was clearly an element of consolation in it."

When I told Peter Hennessy that several English people had told me that "England" ultimately meant for them a green landscape and lovely villages, he expressed no surprise.

The English longing for arcadia—an arcadia that never really existed—has been around for a long time, but I suspect that it really commenced in earnest almost as soon as the industrial revolution started. The English produced the first truly urban society the world had known, but the people who drove on the process of industrialisation could not themselves wait to escape from the city and live in the country, distancing themselves as far as possible from the urban context they had created. Indeed, it has become a historical cliché that the first great English manufacturers had one pre-eminent ambition—to establish themselves as country gentlemen.

This process was given some kind of intellectual sustenance by the unlikely figure of William Cobbett, that greatest of English journalists, with his amazing admixture of radicalism and conservatism. He would have been the last person to approve of industrialists setting themselves up as country squires, yet nobody more than Cobbett gave shape and force to this longing for an agrarian utopia. And after Cobbett came the poets, less robust and polemical, but in their own way just as influential. Tennyson, the greatest Victorian poet, expressed a strong anti-urbanism, as had Wordsworth before him. Both of them, insofar as they were prepared to consider cities favourably at all, could only do so if the city were permeated by "nature".

This strain in English writing became more virulent in the work of Ruskin, the hyper-influential aesthetic pundit. William Morris, another influential Victorian writer, urged his readers to "Forget the spreading of the hideous town/Think rather of the pack horse on the down/And dream of London small and white and clean/The clear Thames bordered by its gardens green."

And thus towards the end of the Victorian era the English, having created the modern city, began trying to recover rural values within it, through careful landscaping and emphasis on that very English device, the urban garden. Suburbs—half urban, half bucolic—were created. Estates like Bedford Park in West London were developed with the intention of disguising the urban truth. The quintessential early suburb, built in this period, consisted of large detached houses with even larger gardens, and roads that looked rustic because they curved and were well planted with broad-leafed trees. Then came the actual garden suburbs, starting with Hampstead Garden Suburb which was laid out early this century. These developments encapsulated the English idea that the town could effectively masquerade as the country; or, to put it another way, that the margins of cities could successfully mutate into rural villages.

Meanwhile, deep in the country itself, what Henry James described as the most perfect and most characteristic of all the great things the English have invented and made part of the credit of their national character—the country house—was enjoying its heyday. James saw such houses as being "well appointed and well filled". Nowadays the urban English may vicariously enjoy the putative glories of the English country house through that characteristic modern English institution, the country house hotel, which perhaps reaches its most refined realisation in the Wolsey Lodge concept; so refined, indeed, that the word "hotel" is carefully avoided. The Wolsey Lodge brochure, "Welcome to an Englishman's Home", from which I have already quoted, talks of "these pleasant country homes, often of historic interest . . . timber-framed Elizabethan manor houses, Georgian mansions, Victorian country rectories and lovingly-restored cottages."

And meanwhile, deep in the cities themselves, the garden still—for those lucky enough to possess one—represented a tiny pocket of country amid the alien cityscape. Shortly after I visited Manchester, the council started knocking down the ugly concrete fortresses of Hulme, a notorious inner city estate that exemplifies most of the planning errors of the sixties. One of the theoretical advantages of high-rise blocks was that they would create a lot of open space for the tenants, as they occupied less real estate. Unfortunately these open spaces became wastelands, scenes of squalor and menace and petty crime. A spokesman for the Hulme tenants said that what people longed for was not common space, but their own gardens, their own private gardens.

But the arcadian ideal must obviously be sought not in the town but in the country. Peter Hennessy suggested to me the continuing political potency—ignored by Mrs Thatcher—of the countryside as symbol of England. And for many English people, this Baldwinesque notion of their green and pleasant land, with its idyllic villages, is the most rewarding image they can summon of their country, vague and half-realised as it is: more potent than the monarchy, or Parliament.

Contemporary rural England lacks the genuinely rustic class—modern peasants, if you will—that you can still find in France or Italy. In England agriculture is for the most part an efficient and very up-to-date business. It is certainly not labour-intensive. The Cheshire farmer I talked with, Stuart Yarwood, loved his farm and his job—but he described an essentially lonely and isolated way of life. And he could not see it continuing for much longer.

Meanwhile the urban English do flock to the country. But then they go to specific places—seaside towns, and other tourist attractions. And when they arrive at, say, Longleat, or Cheddar Gorge, to judge from what I saw, they are content to go where they are directed—and where their money can be judiciously removed from them. There is a sheep-like tendency, a reluctance to explore the hinterlands. Meanwhile vast tracts of England, where the country has not been packaged or dotted with tourist features and facilities, are virtually ignored. Great swathes of Cambridgeshire and Norfolk and Lincolnshire and

Summing Up

Shropshire and Northumbria and West Cumbria—beyond the Lake District—spring to mind in this context.

The English arcadian ideal occasionally encounters the heritage industry, with somewhat comic results. This is perhaps best seen at Edwinstowe, where the Robin Hood industry is centred and where the "Major Oak", which I describe elsewhere and which no doubt once was a great and venerable tree, is now a rather pitiful symbol of England. Yet 350,000 people come to view it each year.

The heritage industry undoubtedly appeals to strong strains in the English character, a longing for the past which allows the present to be bypassed. When you drive south from the Tyne Tunnel, the first thing you encounter are huge signs proclaiming "Catherine Cookson Country". The historical novelist, who purveys a hugely successful brand of South Tyneside nostalgia, is regarded as a more suitable symbol than anything remotely to do with the present (for example, the vast Nissan factory which is the next thing the motorist encounters). And this leads to the trouble with the whole heritage business. An obsession with the past can too easily lead to a fear of the present.

England, as Sue Slipman told me, is struggling to cope with its here-and-now. She thought this was partly because of the loss of externality provided by the Empire. I am sure this is true. For several hundred years England had a colossal impact on the rest of the world. Now it seems hard put to have an impact even on itself.

Another factor is probably the constant packaging of its history, in such a way as to offer an easy escape rather than an understanding of present realities. There also seems to be a disposition to avoid intimate, small-scale recent history in favour of grander, more romantic symbols from the greater past. At Dover I was struck by the contrast between Dover Castle, immaculately maintained by English Heritage, and the more amateurish, almost scruffy little modern transport museum which sat in its shadow, and was under threat of closure. I much preferred the latter.

This fear of the present is evinced in architecture, where the English orthodoxy, alas, is to sneer at the distinguished innovators in their midst, men like Foster and Rogers and Stirling. There is no doubt that the Prince Charles view of modern architecture is the prevailing one in England today, but it seems to me wrong-headed; an example of the veneration of the past to the detriment of the present.

In 1988 the then Home Secretary, the Rt Hon. Douglas Hurd, made an interesting speech which attracted remarkably little publicity. It was essentially a speech on a grand theme, a "condition of England" speech. In the context of modern English politics, it was remarkable for its thoughtfulness, its eloquence and its cerebral ambition. Perhaps that is why it was virtually ignored.

Let me quote from it. "No worthwhile Conservative can be content that, while more and more people live in prosperous suburbs and shires, there remains at the heart of our once great cities—in which much of the wealth of Victorian England was generated—and on gloomy estates isolated on the edges of our cities, a very different world," he said.

"It is a world unattractive to employers; badly designed; blighted by crime; excessively dependent on inadequate or tyrannical local authorities, and, above all, lacking cohesion . . . That is why our policies in the cities are not an extra or a luxury; they treat a disease of the heart.

"But the Government's analysis goes beyond simply identifying social problems with inner cities. . . . In the shires, where crime has traditionally been much lower, it continues to rise apace despite the massive increase in police strength and in the significantly tougher sentences being passed by the courts. The small riot in Lincoln which ushered in the New Year of 1987 is a case in point. There is no question here of deprived, unemployed victims of discrimination, or of something called Thatcherism. In Lincoln that night and in dozens of similar market towns up and down the shires since then we have seen disturbances caused largely by youths who were white, employed, affluent and drunk."

Hurd went on to complain about the lack of responsibility of the churches, and parents. Then he stated: "The fruits of economic success could turn sour unless we can bring back greater social cohesion to our country. Social cohesion is quite different from social equality, indeed the two are ultimately incompatible. But social cohesion alongside the creation of wealth through private enterprise: these are the two conditions of our future progress." (In the context of my earlier remarks contrasting Mrs Thatcher and Baldwin, it was almost as if Hurd was trying to fuse the two Conservative approaches.)

Finally, he suggested that the great achievement of the Victorians had been to create a cohesive society. During the twentieth century the unravelling of that cohesion had gone dangerously far. "During the remainder of the twentieth century, we have set ourselves the task of knitting it together again."

In this speech Hurd was in part attempting to get the Tories off the hook; riots in the shires were not linked to deprivation and thus should not be glibly blamed on Thatcherite policies. But what I found fascinating about the speech was its candid admission that contemporary England—for Hurd was clearly talking about England; for various reasons, Scots do not riot—lacked cohesion. There was also an implication that more riots might come, and that they would not come in the most run-down areas. Hurd was attempting to deal with the "lager lout" phenomenon.

I wrote in the introduction to this book that I found England in a pretty placid state during my tour in 1991; in a rather more placid state than it has been during the shorter tour I undertook in 1977. Nonetheless serious riots did break out later in 1991, in Tyneside and Oxford. Both centred on the vogue for "hotting" —stealing yuppie cars, and delivering them to precocious drivers, many of them under seventeen, on the estates. These drivers would then entertain the assembled lieges—by no means all young people—by various tricks such as "handbrake turns", and then hand the vehicles back to the original thieves who would remove them to obscure roads, strip them and burn them. The riots occurred when the police intervened to stop this new social ritual, which incidentally seems to me to evince another, albeit perverse, aspect of the current English obsession with motor cars.

If I found England placid, it was not because of any great contentment or—to use Douglas Hurd's word—cohesion. Far from it. I was well aware of stresses and strains, divisions and resentments, simmering away beneath the surface of things. But this seemed repressed. It would be absurd and irresponsible to commend "hotting", or approve of it in any way at all, but at least in its bravado and spectacle it represents a release from the vegetation which seems to characterise much of modern English life on the wrong side of the tracks.

When I talked to Ian Johnson on the Langley estate near Rochdale, he told me he was surprised that far more people did not rise up and riot. This deeply compassionate man later wrote to me saying that people on the estate found him critical and aggressive, and felt threatened because of his "discontent at their despair". Such are the complexities of life for those who are moved to discontent, divine or otherwise, by the state of much of modern England. Anyway, Ian had told me that he thought the one thing that did prevent people in many parts of England from rioting was that modern instrument of social control, the video.

And indeed the money spent on video rentals in Britain in 1989 reached the amazing figure of £569 million. There are now signs that the video boom is slowly declining, but that is probably a function of the inexorable rise of satellite television. Go to any housing estate, and one of the most immediately obvious features is the plethora of satellite dishes protruding from the houses. Amid a great fanfare of publicity, BSkyB launched two new film channels just as I was setting out on my tour of England.

The writer Jonathan Raban, looking back on J. B. Priestley's classic *English Journey* of 1933, wrote of English life then that most of it took place out of doors: "You even left your house to go to the lavatory. Out of a job, you stood in full view on the street. Because the slums were usually two storeys high at the most, their streets and backyards became communal living spaces, open to the gaze of visiting writers and photographers. It would have been possible for Priestley to see unemployment at first hand without stepping from his Daimler. It is not so now. Since the 1960s we have moved, or been moved, indoors and upstairs. Unemployment, like so many other features of our social life, has gone private."

Of course, the English have always been a private people; now, one suspects, this tendency is exaggerated, so that they are in danger of becoming a nation of zombies, vegetating privately in front of their tellies. In that respect, and that respect only, you could almost be tempted to regard the odd riot as a healthy aberration.

A year after that speech by Douglas Hurd, another Government Minister, Sir Norman Fowler, who was then in charge of the Department of Employment, announced a major civil service jobs dispersal from London to Cheshire and Yorkshire. He stated: "The quality of life for staff outside London is much better. Travelling is easier. There is a greater sense of community which you cannot conceivably have in London."

Many, perhaps most, people in London would echo that. In the summer of 1991 the Labour Party trumpeted a poll which indicated that as many as 46 per cent of London's citizens were deeply dissatisfied with life in the capital and wanted to move elsewhere. But there were snares for Labour in concentrating too much on policies designed for the problems of the south-east. Labour's strength traditionally lies in the Midlands and, especially, in north England. To win a general election, Labour needed to gain a significant number of seats in the south-east. But Labour could not be seen to be taking its northern votes for granted. A sudden concentration on the problems of London and the south-east might well be seen in the Labour strongholds as at worst a betrayal, and at best a misallocation of political priorities. Labour duly did appoint a special co-ordinator of policy initiatives for the south-east (the MP John Garrett), and the north was not impressed. Meanwhile, later in

1991, London's unemployment levels, for the first time in living memory, became higher than the national average.

In any discussion of England's present and England's future, London looms like some great brooding behemoth. It is a remarkable city, a great cosmopolitan conglomeration whose connections with the rest of England are at times obscure and tenuous. The living there is not easy, and nor is it cheap (London is now officially designated as the second dearest capital city in the EC). The trouble is that the glitzy, yuppie image sticks, despite the statistics suggesting that the realities are very different. There is no generalised English sympathy for London and Londoners; nor is there pride in the capital. There is instead resentment. Partly this is a simple accident of geography; I have long been convinced that England would be a more cohesive country were London situated somewhere towards its physical centre. People who are based in London or elsewhere in the south-east often have a lop-sided view of England's geography. Thus Hugo Young, in his acclaimed biography of Mrs Thatcher, can write that Grantham is in the north of England.

When you move around the north of England, it is not difficult to pick up hostility to London. Let me cite what might seem to be a perverse example of how this can arise. When the on-off transfer of Gazza, the most famous living Englishman, to the Roman club Lazio was being discussed through the summer of 1991, a rather sad light was cast on the story back in the north-east, whence Gazza had come. Newcastle United, his first professional club, stood to gain 10 per cent of the transfer fee if the deal was completed. There was something deeply pathetic about this once-great club, now languishing low in the Second Division and in financial straits, waiting forlornly in the wings for their pickings as the sharp-suited moguls of London and Rome talked megamoney.

So many great English footballers have come from the north-east—the Charlton brothers, Bryan Robson, Chris Waddle and Gazza himself are just a few of the more recent examples. So few of them have lingered for any length of time in their home territory before seeking fame and fortune elsewhere.

Summing Up

Let me conclude this final chapter by recounting the very different perceptions of three very different men on the current condition of England. They have in common at least two attributes: they are outsiders, and they live in London. The first two are outsiders for the very good reason that they are Hungarians: Stephen Vizinczey and Stephen Danos.

Stephen Vizinczey, the best-selling novelist, I have introduced elsewhere in the book. Stephen Danos is a lovely man I have known for many years. In some ways he is more English than the English: he was educated at Westminster, he has a house in Highgate Village, and a cottage in Norfolk; he and his wife Jill send their sons to Harrow. After various spectacular adventures abroad, he built up a successful public relations business in London, sold out, and now he dabbles in consultancy, travels a great deal and enjoys life to the full.

And finally there is Peter Hennessy, whom I have already quoted in this section. Peter is an outsider insofar as he has been the scourge of England's governing establishment, through his relentless exposure of how it actually works. His huge book, simply entitled *Whitehall*, is already a classic; he is now working on a great multi-tome history of modern Britain. He undoubtedly knows as much as anybody about how England works, and how it is governed; he has delved diligently into all the arcane and backstairs places that politicians (in government) and most but not all civil servants prefer to keep private and unexposed, thus incurring the wrath of, among others, Harold Wilson. He has been described, by Professor Ben Pimlott, as a national institution.

First, Stephen Vizinczey:

> I think what is very good about England, although it is also a weakness, is the coolness of the English. They don't worry about anything too much. Opposition to the EC, for example, has never properly got off the ground in England because the English cannot see the EC affecting them very much. The English are incapable of contemplating fundamental or turbulent change, or seeing it coming.

This coolness is partly because the English have never been an occupied country. There are no folk memories, or knowledge of, the horrific changes that can happen so suddenly. There is an understanding, a feeling that nothing can touch the English. Their tolerance is rightly celebrated, but it is based on complacency. They have been spoiled by fate, and they cannot imagine really terrible things happening to their nation.

There is too much equanimity. There is no great outrage at anything. And they are, in some ways, like sheep.

My great theory is that you see people at their best in bad times, in violent times—and it is a long time since the English have experienced such times.

For me, the over-riding symbol of England is Shakespeare. His canon is a treasure house of human wisdom, and all round the world people reckon that England is Shakespeare. But Shakespeare lived in bad, and dangerous times. He knew what many modern English do not know. Shakespeare will be more enduring than the English Parliament. He is central to civilisation, and to what England is to the world.

The best part of England, where I go to raise my spirits, is the South Bank. I don't know of anywhere else, including the US and all the Continent, where there is so much devoted to good culture. To me what is specifically good and English is that stretch of London.

On to Stephen Danos:

The great English characteristic is the ability to leave you alone, to let you live your own life. My mother said to me that England was the best place to be poor. There is a basic decency here which I have never found anywhere else. Against that, the English are extraordinarily hypocritical. They have a distinct streak of 'holier than thou'.

Whether, in forty years' time, it will be as nice a place, I don't know. There seems to be an enormous deterioration. France, for example, is changing a great deal less. Parental responsibility is missing in England. The Continentals have been much better at maintaining the family unit.

Summing Up

Here you have few communities of the kind you still find in France. I know of no English village which does things not for tourists, but for its own people. In France it is usually the other way round.

I think English people who live well away from London have a slightly false impression of what Londoners think of them. There is an aggression up the country. People say 'I come from Yorkshire' as if that really mattered. It's almost like an inferiority complex. Jill comes from Accrington in Lancashire—I can't pretend it's a nice place. It's not, it's an arsehole. If you live there you either laugh it off, or you claim that's where real people live, unlike London.

When I return to England from abroad I am, these days, struck by the shabbiness. But I also immediately realise how much better, how much safer, how much more courteous the driving is here. I'm always glad to be back . . . other things do irritate me: how difficult it is to eat well for the right money, for example, though that has improved with the influx of foreigners . . . I think it's a decent country, the most decent country in the world, it allows you to live decently with a fair degree of privacy.

And finally, some brief comments from Peter Hennessy:

If London is a succession of villages, then England is a succession of parishes. The parochialism is very, very intense. The English are a most insular, and a most parochial, people. For such a small country, in terms of space, there is a deep variety: the climate changes rapidly, as do the accents . . . there is a sense of real remoteness in many parts of England.

Although we were the first urban society, we never really produced proper urban values. The compensations of living in an old, old country are huge. You go into an old English parish church and you see the list of vicars going back for hundreds and hundreds of years: in that sense we do not need a heritage industry, it's in our very bones. This is in a way exceptionally consoling.

Younger nations rapidly become neurotic when they hit a bad patch; the English can live with fifty bad years, and not get too bothered.

There we are. There is an element of impertinence in seeking to draw conclusions at the end of a journey. I recall meeting in 1977 a marvellous hotelier who had decided to throw out her French cookbooks and concentrate on good English cooking. She told me about how one of "her girls" had made a syllabub and served it with a cherry on top. "I saw red," she said (not unnaturally) "and I told her: 'You are not in Lyons now, dear'!" Trying to sum up a series of variegated impressions can be rather like sticking a cherry on a syllabub: a redundant gesture of vulgarity.

Anyway, England is a uniquely localised country, and it is dangerous to generalise too much. All I will say is that I do reckon that it faces growing dislocation; that in some ways it is in danger of falling apart. This is partly a function of that very localised quality; but these days there is no great force or institution or dynamic holding the disparate parts together. England has, however, faced such dangers many times before. The English are superb at avoiding revolutions, at reforming their institutions, and at renewing their national life. But as a Scot, I do sense that England's nationhood is mainly behind it, while Scotland's lies ahead. I have also to admit that we will be doing very well indeed if we do half as well as the English have already done.